W9-ADF-659

INSTRUMENTAL
MUSIC

Da Capo Press Music Reprint Series
GENERAL EDITOR
FREDERICK FREEDMAN
VASSAR COLLEGE

INSTRUMENTAL MUSIC

A Conference at
Isham Memorial Library
Harvard University
May 4, 1957

EDITED BY

DAVID G. HUGHES

DA CAPO PRESS · NEW YORK · 1972

Library of Congress Cataloging in Publication Data

Isham Library Conference, Harvard University, 1957.
   Instrumental music.
   (Da Capo Press music reprint series)
   Original ed. issued as vol. 1 of Isham Library papers series.
   CONTENTS: Introductory address, by A. T. Merritt.—Dance tunes of the
fifteenth century, by O. Kinkeldey.—Problems of authenticity in eighteenth-
century music, by H. C. R. Landon. [etc.]
   1. Music—Congresses. 2. Musicology—Addresses, essays, lectures. 3. Instru-
mental music—History and criticism. I. Hughes, David G., ed.
ML38.C17I86   1972   785   70-166094
ISBN 0-306-70273-8

This Da Capo Press edition of *Instrumental Music* is an unabridged republica-
tion of the first edition published in Cambridge, Massachusetts, in 1959. It is
reprinted by special arrangement with Harvard University Press.

© 1959 by the President and Fellows of Harvard College

Published by Da Capo Press, Inc.
A Subsidiary of Plenum Publishing Corporation
227 W. 17 St., New York, New York 10011

INSTRUMENTAL MUSIC

Isham Library Papers I

INSTRUMENTAL MUSIC

A Conference at
Isham Memorial Library
May 4, 1957

EDITED BY

DAVID G. HUGHES

HARVARD UNIVERSITY PRESS, 1959
CAMBRIDGE, MASSACHUSETTS

Distributed in Great Britain by Oxford University Press, London

Library of Congress Catalog Card Number 59–9275
Printed in the United States of America

PREFACE

On May 4, 1957, a group of some thirty-four scholars from the northeastern part of the United States met together in the Isham Memorial Library of Harvard University to hear and discuss four papers dealing with various phases of the topic "Instrumental Music." This meeting, sponsored by the American Council of Learned Societies, was the first in what is expected to be a series of Isham Library Conferences, and it was especially fitting that Mrs. Ralph Isham, to whose patronage the library owes its continued existence, should have been present as an honored guest.

The program of the day's activities was a simple one. Two papers (those of Dr. Kinkeldey and Dr. Landon) were presented and discussed at a morning session, and there followed a luncheon for the participants at the Signet Society of Harvard University. The papers of Professor Werner and Professor Piston, and the discussion of them, occupied the afternoon session. This ended the primary business of the conference, but, since it was felt that no gathering devoted to musical scholarship could wholly dispense with the living presence of music in sound, one further item was added to the program: a service of Vespers at the nearby Monastery of St. Mary and St. John (of the Episcopal Society of St. John the Evangelist), adorned with Sarum plain song and service music of William Byrd.

The present volume makes available to the general scholarly public the proceedings of the conference. All four papers are, of course, included, and, since both of the sessions were entirely recorded on tape, it has also been possible to present the discussions. It is hoped that the publication of all this material will (in addition to its considerable intrinsic importance) stimulate the organization of future conferences, not only at the Isham Library, but elsewhere as well; and thus contribute to the exchange, both formal and informal, of ideas and achievements in musical scholarship.

A few words concerning the presentation of the material may be useful. The papers are, on the whole, printed here much as they were originally delivered: the authors have generally made only necessary additions of documentation and musical examples, together with minor changes in wording. It is obvious, however, that the discussion could not be so simply treated. Even the most formal conversation has a way of sounding inappropriately casual in print, and there were, moreover, unavoidable repetitions and deviations from logical order in the course of the day's proceedings. As a result, the discussions as printed here differ to a certain extent from the verbatim transcripts of the tapes which served as their basis. Some condensations were made, the conversational style was altered slightly in the direction of formality, and a few changes in order were introduced in order to bring together material on the same topic. Nevertheless, the speakers' wording was retained in all essential matters, and every effort was made to preserve the exact meaning in passages where changes were made. The revisions have not, in most cases, been resubmitted to the speakers, and thus the responsibility for any distortion of views in the discussions is that of the editor. The editor is also responsible for the explanatory footnotes in the discussion sections (the notes in the papers are, of course, the work of the authors).

David G. Hughes

Cambridge, Massachusetts

CONTENTS

INTRODUCTORY ADDRESS

A. Tillman Merritt

As Curator of the Isham Library it is my duty and my pleasure to welcome you to this conference and to say a few words by way of introduction.

Some years ago, with the encouragement of Dr. Archibald T. Davison, Mr. Ralph Isham began at Harvard a library of music to be played on the organ in the Memorial Church. At the death of Mr. Isham it was decided by Mrs. Isham that she would turn this collection into a memorial to her husband, and that she would expand it into a library of source materials for research in music. As a result of her decision and her constant enthusiasm and support it has grown to its present size, and it is now an indispensable part of the musical library resources of Harvard University.

The orientation of the Isham Memorial Library, as distinguished from the Loeb Music Library and the Houghton Library with its musical treasures, is toward microfilms and photostats of musical manuscripts and early musical prints. With its growth each year has naturally come a much increased use of these materials both by Harvard staff and students and by visitors. Harvard is very proud of the Isham Memorial Library and most grateful to Mrs. Isham not only for putting at our disposal such a body of otherwise rather inaccessible materials but for her generosity in providing for its constant growth.

Since the Isham Memorial Library has proved so valuable it was decided, upon the suggestion of Professor John Ward, to organize a scholars' conference in this vicinity, possibly at the Isham Library itself. An approach was made to the American Council of Learned Societies through its chairman, Professor Howard Mumford Jones, to see if the Council would be interested in sponsoring such a conference. The

Council's Committee on Musicology, under the chairmanship of Mr. Edward N. Waters, welcomed this opportunity: it was decided that the conference would be regional in nature and that it would be confined to those scholars who would participate directly, either through reading papers or through prepared discussions. The planners were left a completely free hand to shape the details as they saw fit. It was a matter of great pride that we could present this conference under such distinguished sponsorship.

Although the Isham Library long since has grown far beyond its original purpose of providing music to be played on the organ, it is possible that its holdings are still most numerous in the field of keyboard and instrumental music. This (in turn) influenced the direction the conference would take. As a beginning it was decided to direct our attention to instrumental music, and not to confine it to a small period. This decision is reflected in the papers which follow. A lack of concentration on a smaller period in this particular conference will, it is hoped, be compensated by its broader range, and by the inclusion among the speakers of a composer whose instrumental compositions and books have gained acceptance among musicologists as well as practical musicians and the general public.

Special thanks are due to Professor John Ward for his invaluable advice from the first days of planning the conference, and to Professor Nino Pirrotta and Dr. David Hughes for their help and suggestions. The conference is also indebted to Father Granville M. Williams of the Society of St. John the Evangelist for his cooperation in presenting the Vespers Service, and to Mr. Claudio Spies for his direction of the music on that occasion. Finally, I must also thank profoundly the speakers and the panelists under the masterful chairmanship of Dr. Curt Sachs for the good will, time, and scholarly work they have contributed to the conference.

DANCE TUNES OF THE
FIFTEENTH CENTURY

Otto Kinkeldey

SOURCES

It is now well known that by the second half of the fifteenth century the educated and aristocratic classes of Italy had developed a highly complex and sophisticated style of drawing-room and ballroom dancing. A number of masters and teachers of this art had established reputations at all the courts of northern Italy, at Venice and Florence, and even as far south as Naples.

These masters laid down their ideas on the theory and practice of their art in treatises which are generally cast in the same bipartite form. The first part contains a theoretical and aesthetic discussion concerning the nature of the art of dancing and its significance as a courtly accomplishment, together with a general description and classification of the types of dance steps used in performance, something of the time relations among the steps, and of the relative tempi of the music that goes with each type of step. Sometimes a series of tests for a good dancer is included.

The second part of such a treatise is given over to a series of choreographic descriptions of a larger or smaller number of specific dances, each bearing its own title. The title is sometimes a proper name or a place name, and sometimes a poetical or fanciful term. In a few rare cases, the name indicates a dramatic content or a representational quality of the dance; but, as a rule, the descriptions leave us with the impression that the dances were mostly conventional ballroom movements with no programmatic significance.

In the second (practical) parts of the Italian treatises, the dances are divided into two groups. The first contains the type called *bassa danza* (basse dance), described as "The Queen of Measures" — a slow, sedate dance, without brusque movements. It is a stepped or paced dance, and is supposed to avoid the leaping or hopping which results when the feet are lifted high in the air (the basse dance descriptions, however, sometimes show exceptions to this rule: see below, p. 13). The second group of descriptions contains nothing but so-called *balli* (sometimes *balletti*). In these, the relatively even, homogeneous movement of the *bassa danza* is replaced by a sometimes startling variety of figures and rhythms, reducible to four basic types, which differ from each other in tempo as already described in the theoretical parts of the treatises. These four types — the *bassa danza*, *quadernaria* (often called the *saltarello tedesco*), the *saltarello* (also known as the *passo brabante* and, in Spain, as the *alta danza*), and the *piva* — are used in varying combinations to make up the *balli*. They will be further discussed in connection with the music.[1]

Four of the Italian treatise manuscripts contain musical notation, all (with the exception of music for three basse dances) for *ballo* tunes. The notation gives the tunes only: there are no chordal or polyphonic settings. Bar lines are absent except to separate the various movements or strains of the *balli*. The number of such strains varies from two (in the dance *Voltate in ça Rosina*) [2] to nine (*Prisoniera*) or ten (*Sobria*). *Tesara* seems to have thirteen strains — or at any rate there are thirteen bar lines. These *ballo* tunes, and not the choreography, are the main object of the present investigation.

At this point it is proper to point out that we know something about a similar dance activity in France and Burgundy during the period in question. We have two French or Burgundian documents which deal with the courtly dances of these more westerly regions more concisely than the Italians do with their dances (perhaps because the French style of the basse dance seems to have been a less elaborate performance than

[1] A survey of the art of dancing in the fifteenth century may be found in Chapter VII of Professor Curt Sachs' *World History of the Dance*, English Edition (New York, 1937).

[2] The music for all of the dances may be found, in alphabetical arrangement, in the appendix of this volume.

the Italian). The first of these two French sources is a manuscript of the later fifteenth century now in the Royal Library at Brussels. It was edited in facsimile by Ernest Closson under the title, *Le Manuscrit dit des Basses Dances de la Bibliothèque de Bourgogne*.[3] Many years later there was discovered in the Library of the Royal College of Physicians of London a still unique copy of an incunabulum bearing the title *L'Art et Instruction de Bien Dancer*, printed in Paris by Michiel Tholouze. Its date has not been definitely established: a manuscript date, 1488, at the end of the unicum, is regarded as possible, although not certain. We may, however, be sure that the book was printed in or before 1496, for in that year Tholouze (or Toulouze) moved from the address of "The Stag's Horn" printed in the colophon. This book was published in facsimile with a preface by Victor Scholderer in London (1936).

Both of these sources cover much the same ground. Each has a brief theoretical introduction, and each deals mainly with the basse dance. Many paragraphs are identical, although they are not arranged in the same order. Neither source is wholly accurate: the Brussels manuscript contains a few obvious scribal errors; and the printing in Toulouze (a double printing of black notes on four red lines) is very poor. The register is often inexact, but it can frequently be corrected by comparison with Brussels. The peculiar notation of these two sources will concern us later (p. 12).

Mention of the French dance treatises inevitably calls to mind the question of the possible relationships between the French basse dance tunes with, on the one hand, the polyphonic chanson, and, on the other, with the music of the Italian *balli* or *basse danze*. A number of scholars (Van den Borren, Gurlitt, Hertzmann, Pirro, and Ranke with Mueller-Blattau) have discovered resemblances between the French basse dances and polyphonic French chansons of the same period; but no direct and complete parallel between one of the monodic dance tunes and a polyphonic version was known until Manfred Bukofzer published a two-voice setting of a so-called basse dance "tenor," *Il Re di Spagna*,[4]

[3] Brussels, 1912.
[4] "A Polyphonic Basse Dance of the Renaissance," in *Studies in Mediaeval and*

which is given in one Italian source, and, with the title *Casulle la novele*, in Toulouze (it is not in Brussels). Otto Gombosi recognized *Casulle* as a misprint for Castille.[5]

The two-part setting is found in Manuscript 431 of the Communal Library of Perugia, in which the notes of the tune (notated in Toulouze in a series of black breves, as is the case for all French basse dances, but in white semibreves in the Italian source) are used evenly, one to a measure, as a *cantus firmus* in the usual Renaissance style, with a florid upper part. The tune itself proves to be a melody known over a large part of western Europe under the name *La Spagna*. Gombosi, in the long and unusually important preface to his edition of the Capirola Lute-book,[6] traces its history through more than two centuries, listing thirty-three real polyphonic settings, together with several other groups of settings in which *La Spagna* is used as a *cantus firmus* for counterpoint exercises (these include in all 208 didactic examples).

This connection between *La Spagna* and polyphonic music of the Renaissance expands the known relationships of the dance tunes in one direction. The present study will extend them in another, as our discussion of the Italian *ballo* tunes will offer a hitherto unnoticed direct parallel between one of the Italian *balli* and a piece found in both Brussels and Toulouze (see below, p. 22).

After this brief excursus on the two French sources, we may return to the Italian dance literature. The Italian sources are more numerous than the French: until recently, eight Italian manuscripts dealing with the subject were known, five in Italian libraries, and three in the National Library in Paris. All of these are discussed in this writer's study "A Jewish Dancing Master of the Renaissance, Guglielmo Ebreo." [7]

Renaissance Music (New York, 1950), pp. 190–216. In a recent posthumous publication of a paper by Bukofzer, "Changing Aspects of Medieval and Renaissance Music" (*Musical Quarterly,* XLIV, 1958, 15–17) this scholar makes several additions to the list of pieces which he considers polyphonic settings of basses dances.

[5] Bukofzer, "A Polyphonic Basse Dance," p. 197.

[6] *Compositione di Messer Vincenzo Capirola. Lute-book circa 1517* (Neuilly-sur-Seine, 1955).

[7] In *Studies in Jewish Bibliography and Related Subjects, in Memory of Abraham Solomon Freidus* (New York, 1929), pp. 329–372. Also published separately.

The bibliography of twenty-seven items which concludes this study was expanded by Bukofzer [8] to the imposing total of seventy-seven entries, chiefly by the addition of the more recent literature which the growing interest in the subject has produced.

In addition, we may now add to the eight manuscripts heretofore known a ninth codex, still unpublished, containing another version of the treatise of Guglielmo Ebreo. This is a redaction, presumably by the Giorgio who names himself on a preliminary leaf as the copyist or possessor. It contains no music, but is rich in dance descriptions. The manuscript is now in the possession of Dr. Walter Toscanini of New York.[9]

The richest of the Italian sources for dance descriptions is the Guglielmo codex in the Communal Library of Siena. It contains twenty-eight basse dances and thirty-two *balli*, but no music. Curzio Mazzi published this treatise in 1914 in the journal *Bibliofilia*.[10]

Aside from mere listings in catalogues, the earliest attempt to draw attention to this dance literature was made by Adrien de la Fage, who, in 1864, published a condensed description of the contents of a Guglielmo treatise in the Magliabecchiana Collection, now in the National Library in Florence.[11] In 1873, Francesco Zambrini published the whole of this version. Since then, other versions of Guglielmo have been published in part, as well as the whole treatise of Antonio Cornazano (this last by Curzio Mazzi).[12]

The names of four authors are associated with these treatises. The earliest is Domenico da Ferrara, sometimes called Domenico Piacentino. All the later writers speak of Domenico in terms of the highest respect, as their master and teacher, but we have no work actually bearing Domenico's name as author. One of the three Paris manuscripts (*fonds*

[8] In the essay "A Polyphonic Basse Dance of the Renaissance," mentioned above, note 4.

[9] I am deeply indebted to Dr. Toscanini for his generous willingness to allow me to use this manuscript as well as his microfilms and their photographic enlargements of the three manuscripts in the Bibliothèque Nationale in Paris, and also the Siena codex of Guglielmo Ebreo.

[10] Anno XVI (Florence, 1914), pp. 185–209.

[11] *Essais de diphthérographie musicale* (Paris, 1864), II, 195–200.

[12] *Bibliofilia*, Anno XVII (Florence, 1916), pp. 1–30.

ital. 972) seems to be a report of Domenico's teachings by an unnamed writer, who speaks of Domenico in the third person, as *el spectable e nobele cavaliero Domenigino piacentino.*

Two other authors are Guglielmo Ebreo and Giovanni Ambrosio. One of the Paris treatises is ascribed to Guglielmo, another to Giovanni Ambrosio. But, in point of fact, the two works are almost identical. Wherever the name of Guglielmo occurs in the first, the name of Giovanni Ambrosio is substituted in the second; and the dance choreographies assigned in the first to Guglielmo are in the second allocated to Giovanni. With an individual whose works were as well known and widespread as Guglielmo's, this could hardly have been a barefaced attempt at forgery or deception. The assumption that the two names really referred to one and the same person seems to be the most logical explanation. It has been suggested by Carlo Antonio Vianello [13] that Guglielmo became converted to Christianity and changed his name, but Vianello offers no documentary evidence. The Giorgio of Dr. Toscanini's manuscript applies the expression "che fù ebreo" not only to Guglielmo, but to Domenico and Giovanni Ambrosio as well.

The fourth dance treatise writer was the Italian man of letters and courtier, Antonio Cornazano (1429–1484), who, in his younger days, wrote a treatise very much like the others.

DANCE TUNES

We turn now to the actual music. Of the sources in Italian libraries only one (that of Cornazano) contains music, while all three of the Paris manuscripts contain some. Altogether, we are made acquainted with twenty-six dance melodies, all noted, as has been stated, as monodic tunes. Only three of these are basse dances in the stricter sense of the term, all the rest being *balli*. The basse dances occur only in Cornazano, who, having scattered through his treatise the tunes of seven *balli*, gives at the end three *Tenori da bassedançe et saltarelli, gli megliori et più usitati di gli altri.*

Guglielmo, in the theoretical portion of his treatise, throws some light on the manner in which these tunes were written. The composer of a

[13] *Teatri, spettacoli, musiche a Milano nei secoli scorsi* (Milan, 1941), p. 56.

new *ballo* must first decide which of the two scales (*chiave*) he is going to use: that of *B-molle* or that of *B-quadro*.[14] Then he must find, *colla sua fantasia*, the *tenore overo il suono*. After this, we must assume, came the invention or application of the dance steps. In his chapter on *misura* Guglielmo insists, while speaking of the instrumental music which accompanies the dance, that the time values of all measures must be alike for the heavy (*il pieno*) and the light part (*il vuoto*) of the measure, and that the *tenore* and *contratenore* [!] must be measured alike.

The Ballo tunes

1.	Amoroso			D			12.	Leoncello	A	C	D G
2.	Anello	A					13.	Ligiadra	A		G
3.	Belfiore			D			14.	Marchesana	A		D G
4.	Belreguardo	A	C	D G			15.	Mercantia	A	C	D G
5.	Colonnese	A		G			16.	Petit Vriens	A		
6.	La Figlia Guil-ielmino		C	D			17.	Pizoccara	A		D G
							18.	Prisoniera	A		D G
7.	Gelosia	A		D G			19.	Sobria		C	D
8.	Gioioso (Rostiboli)	A					20.	Spero	A		G
9.	Giove (= Jupiter)	A	C	D G			21.	Tesara			D
10.	Gratioso	A		G			22.	Verzeppe		C	D
11.	Ingrata	A		D G			23.	Voltate in ça Rosina	A		

Cornazano's *tenori* for *bassedanze*

24. Tenore del Re di Spagna
25. Cançon de pifari dicto el Ferrarese
26. Tenore Collinetto

A = Giovanni Ambrosio (Paris, Bib. nat. *fonds ital.* 476); C = Cornazano; D = Domenico (*fonds ital.* 972); G = Guglielmo (*fonds ital.* 973).

The above table lists all of the dance tunes known from the Italian treatises (including, of course, those in Paris). It is in some respects an improvement on the table in my Guglielmo Ebreo study,[15] for it includes two items which at that time escaped the photographer,

---

[14] For a discussion of the scales, see below, Clefs and Key Signatures, p. 18.
[15] See above, note 7.

or were omitted from my order for photocopies. There is one new tune — *Tesara* — and a new parallel version for *Verzeppe*.

Four *ballo* tunes are found in all the musical sources, five in three, seven in two, and seven in one. All of these tunes are printed in the musical appendix to this study, arranged in alphabetical order for easy reference and study. All parallel versions are given in score in the original notation, and added to these is a tentative transcription (in some puzzling places very tentative indeed). Many modern transcribers of fifteenth-century music prefer to reduce the note values in their transcriptions to one fourth of the original value. Our transcription follows an older practice of reducing the notes by one half. This gives the transcriptions only a somewhat modern appearance, but it greatly facilitates the continual comparison of the transcriptions with the originals, back and forth, measure by measure, for which the scores are intended.

The transcriptions are an attempt to treat the tunes from the musical standpoint alone, with only occasional references to the choreographical descriptions. Many of the notations seem to fall very easily into clear and logical musical dance rhythms. As has just been mentioned, the notation in a few cases does not yield so easily to this treatment. *Belfiore* is a case in point. How far these rhythms will eventually have to be modified or corrected depends on the results of deeper, continued study of the difficult theoretical explanations. The sometimes conflicting time signatures found in the notations are discussed on pages 16 to 17.

Many of the choreographical descriptions give not the slightest indication of the nature of the musical measure. Other descriptions do give one or more such hints, but they are by no means always clear enough to enable one to identify the actual strain of the music to which reference is made. Wherever the reference is reasonably clear (as is always the case where the reference is to the opening strain) the applicable remark has been added to the proper version of the tune in the musical supplement. In other cases, however, it seems impossible, at the present stage of our understanding of the descriptions, to be sure which part of the music is intended. In such instances, the supplement contains no mention of the references.

At this point we may insert another correction of my Guglielmo study. Cornazano calls his basse dance melodies *tenori*, while the *ballo* tunes in Cornazano and in the three Paris manuscripts generally follow the title of the dance by the words *in canto*; as, for example, "*Anello in canto*." I assumed that the word *canto* had the same significance here as it has in common usage of the period, which applied it to a voice of higher tessitura (synonymous with *soprano*), and that this indicated a contrast between the lower tenors of the basse dances and the higher position of *ballo* tunes. The same assumption has been made by other writers as well (Gombosi, Bukofzer, and Torrefranca). A closer study reveals, however, that this interpretation is erroneous. Besides the simple form of title with *in canto* we sometimes find the title *in canto a sonare*. Giovanni Ambrosio, at the end of his index of dance choreographies (fol. 6ʳ), indexes his musical appendix with the words, *Li balli notati per ragione di canto*. The Paris Domenico codex (*fonds ital.* 972) provides the necessary clue: it gives the music of the dance with the title and *in canto*; and this is then followed immediately by the choreography of the same dance with the title followed by the words *in ballo* or *a ballo*. The word *canto*, therefore, means merely "music." *Ingrata in canto* means "*Ingrata* in music," and *Ingrata in ballo* means "*Ingrata* in dance steps." The contrast is not between the higher and lower positions of the tune, but between the music and the choreographic description.

The sources give little information as to the composers of the tunes. The only significant statement is made in the Paris Domenico manuscript (*fonds ital.* 972, fol. 7ʳ), where we find the words: *La infrascripte dançe sono composto cusi il canto come le parole per lo Spectabile & egregio cavagliero, Misser Domenico da piasença, salvo che il canto de la figlia guilielmino che e ballatta francese, et sopra esso canto el dicto cavalier ha composto i dicti [due] balli.*[16] Here we have one piece of evidence suggesting a direct connection between France and Italy, and

[16] "The dances written below were composed, the tunes as well as the words, by the most honorable and distinguished gentleman, Misser Domenico da Piacenza; except the tune of *La Figlia Guilielmo*, which is a French ballata; and on this tune the aforesaid gentleman has composed the steps of the [two] *balli* given here."

there are a few other indications of the same sort. In his index list (fols. 4ᵛ and 6ʳ) Giovanni Ambrosio enters a *bassa danza Borges francese*, and at the end of the list a *ballo francese Amoroso* and another *ballo francese Petit riense*. Domenico's *Petite rose* has a French name, and Mrs. Mabel Dolmetsch (below, page 22) claims *Venus* also as a French name, for in Italian it should be *Venere*.

NOTATION

The first problem which faces us as we study this music is the question of notation. When the Brussels basse dance manuscript was first made known (and, later, the Toulouze incunabulum), scholars were puzzled by the manner of notation of these French basse dances. They are almost all written in the French sources in long series of black breves without bars, and each is accompanied by an actual count of the number of notes in the tune, as well as the number of *mesures*. The word *mesure* does not here signify musical measures or bars, but is applied to certain typical, conventional groups of dance steps, each consisting, usually, of from seven to eleven steps.

There is also for each piece what we might call a tablature of dance steps, in which each step is represented by the initial letter of its name. (For the French step *démarche*, we find an unusual sign which is nothing else but an old form of the letter "r" sometimes used by the incunabula printers as an alternative to the commoner form. In the French dance tablatures it is borrowed from Italian terminology, being the initial letter of the term *ripresa*, the Italian equivalent of the *démarche*.) The French letter tablatures are replaced in the Italian treatises by the often profuse, complicated, and in places really unintelligible dance choreographies which constitute the whole of the second (or practical) part of a treatise. They will undoubtedly be cleared up some day by patient choreographical specialists.

The Italian musical notation is different. As has been said, Cornazano's three basse dance tenors are noted, not in black breves, but in white semibreves. All of the Italian musical notators write in the white notation which was in general use in the second half of the fifteenth century (although it began earlier). The notation of the *ballo* tunes is, however, strikingly different from that of the basse dances. There are, in general, few *longae*, and those which do appear ordinarily mark the end of a piece or of a strain (there is an exception in the fourth strain of *Gratioso*). There are also occasional white breves, but by far the greater portion of the *ballo* tunes is notated in white semibreves and white minims. Smaller values appear more sparingly: there are some black (rarely white) semiminims, and *fusae* appear in Giovanni Ambrosio's version of *Gratioso*, and in Giovanni's and Guglielmo's versions of *Mercantia*.

This difference in notation accurately reflects the differences in formal structure and rhythm which separate the *ballo* tunes from the basse dance melodies. The even succession of black breves in the French sources (or of white semibreves in Cornazano's tenors) would seem to indicate a uniform type of dance movement from beginning to end, while the more varied notation of the *balli* naturally agrees with the greater diversity of steps within the whole dance. In general, the choreographic descriptions seem to preserve this distinction of character between the two types, but there are, nevertheless, a fair number of directions in the Italian basse dance descriptions for the insertion of *saltarello* steps in a *bassa danza*. Usually two or four measures of *saltarello* are called for; several times the choreography requires six; and Domenico's *Mignotta* calls for twelve. Both Giovanni (in *Principessa* and *Caterva*) and Guglielmo (*Principessa*) also prescribe the *saltarello tedesco* or *quadernaria*: the tunes of these dances have not been preserved.

Just as the Italian basse dances occasionally admit passages in other steps, so, conversely, do the *balli* contain sections in basse dance. Ordinarily, the occurrence of a series of white semibreves in a *ballo* indicates such a passage (appearing in our transcriptions as dotted half notes in 6/4 measures). The basse dance is also often noted in true six-part measures with the ♩♩ ♩♩ rhythm. When the even series of semibreves is used, the scribes sometimes group the notes into clear groups of three or four, corresponding to the *botte* or strokes on the instrument, which are occasionally mentioned in the theoretical parts of the treatises.

The relative time value of the Italian basse dance notation poses some problems. Gombosi (in the Capirola preface and elsewhere) assumed that the white semibreves of an Italian basse dance (or of a passage of basse dance in a *ballo*) should be read like the black breves of the French notation, thus doubling the Italian values. There is some authority for this. Cornazano [17] tells us that in the imperial measure of the basse dance *ogni nota si radoppia, et le tre vagliono sei, et le sei dodici*. It is not always easy, however, to apply this rule to the ballo notation of the scribes. The transcriptions in the musical appendix make no attempt to do so, but merely present the basse dance passages in the same manner as the rest of the dances. Thus, both in the originals and in the transcriptions, a basse dance and a *saltarello* often look alike on paper: the difference would have to be made by the player and dancer in the actual performance.

The theoretical discussions in some of the treatises tell us a little more concerning this problem. They give us the relative time or tempo values of the four standard dance types. Unfortunately they give no information which would enable us to fix an absolute time value that could be expressed in a metronome notation.[18]

[17] Mazzi, *Bibliofilia*, Anno XVII, p. 29.

[18] The pertinent passages are found in Domenico (Paris, *ital.* 972, fol. 4ᵛ), Guglielmo (Siena, L.V. 29, fols. 30ᵛ to 31ʳ), and Cornazano (Mazzi, *Bibliofilia*, Anno XVII, pp. 14–15). The Domenico explanation is quite clear and is accompanied by a tabular arrangement of the four dance types in a vertical column with the *bassa danza* at the top and the *piva* at the bottom, and with brief notes on each dance. It has been translated into French by Laure Fonta in her edition of Jehan Tabourot's *Orchésographie* (Paris, 1888, p. xix). An English translation of the diagram and of the whole passage that precedes it may be found in Mrs. Mabel Dolmetsch's *Dances of Spain and Italy from 1400 to 1600* (London, 1954, pp. 5–7). Cornazano also gives a diagram. It is in the form of a ladder with steps or rungs which increase as we ascend. The short-time *piva* is the lowest step, the slow *bassa danza* is at the top. Cornazano gives no arithmetical numbers for the relative time values, but indicates that his diagram is drawn to a definite scale. This seems to be the case, for, in the diagram as drawn in the Vatican manuscript, and in Mazzi's photo-reproduction, the varying lengths of the rungs of the ladder seem to conform fairly accurately with the numbers given by Domenico. The *piva* rung is just about half as long as the *bassa danza* rung. In Cornazano's later explanation of how the steps of one dance may be adapted to the music of each of the three other types, he sometimes uses numbers which

The explanations may be condensed as follows. The dignified *bassa danza*, "The Queen of Measures," is the slowest. The *quadernaria* is one-sixth faster than the *bassa danza* (*per distantia de tempo a più strecta de la bassadanza uno sesto*), or, it reduces the bassa danza by one sixth (*uno sesto cala della bassa danza*). The *saltarello* reduces the tempo by another sixth, that is, by one third of the *bassa danza*; while the *piva* reduces the tempo of the *bassa danza* by three sixths or one half. Thus six measures of *quadernaria* take as much time as five measures of *bassa danza*; six measures of *saltarello* take as much time as four of *bassa danza*; and six measures of *piva* are equal to three of *bassa danza*. The *piva* is twice as fast as the *bassa danza*.

If we wish to apply these ratios to the barred measures adopted in our experimental transcriptions, we must remember that, according to the treatise writers, each measure consists of two parts, an accented or heavy beat (*il pieno*) and an unaccented or weak beat (*il vuoto*). The beat of the *bassa danza* and usually of the *saltarello* is represented in our rhythmically reduced transcription by ♩.; and ♩ is the beat of the *quadernaria* and often, though by no means always, of the *piva*. If, merely for the sake of arithmetical convenience, and not as an actually established metronome measure, we choose 60 and 120 as our limiting numbers, we arrive at:

Bassa danza	♩.	= M.M.60
Quadernaria	♩	= M.M.72
Saltarello	♩.	= M.M.90
Piva	♩ or ♩.	= M.M.120

Professor Curt Sachs, approaching the problem from another angle,[19] concludes "that the tempo of the basse dance must be set at 𝅝 or ♩ = M.M. 40." His series from *bassa danza* to *piva* would then be 40, 48, 60, 80.

---

agree with Domenico's. The explanation given in the Siena codex of Guglielmo is an incomplete and very corrupt version of Domenico.

[19] *World History of the Dance*, English Edition (New York, 1937), p. 318. It should be noted that Professor Sachs would reduce the original note values to one fourth, not to one half as in our transcriptions.

In closing these general remarks on notation we might call attention to some unusual notation cases. In *Gratioso*, for example, the fourth strain consists of an unusual series of seven white *longae*, to be played twice. It is undoubtedly a basse dance passage, although it is not so named in the description. In *Marchesana*, the fourth strain (a basse dance passage of thirteen measures) is noted entirely in white breves by Giovanni, while the versions of Domenico and Guglielmo present it in white semibreves. In *Prisoniera*, the first five strains in Giovanni's version are written mostly in breves and semibreves; Domenico and Guglielmo write the same melodies, transposed a fourth higher, in semibreves and minims

MENSURAL SIGNS

The *tempus* or time signatures present a problem by themselves. They are, in the first place, neither consistently present nor consistently absent. Eight of the dances have no mensural sign whatever; five have no sign at the beginning, but introduce one or more in a later strain or strains. Ten begin with a sign and have frequent changes in later strains. The absence of a mensural sign does not always lead to problems in transcription: the meter and rhythm often seem perfectly clear without such aid. In many cases the mere grouping of the notes on the lines of the staff seems to indicate a definite rhythmical structure, as in the case of the grouped semibreves mentioned above (p. 13). *Belreguardo* and *Colonnese* are examples of this, and there are many more besides.

The mensural signs commonly used in the *ballo* notation are four in number: (1) the full circle with dot (*tempus perfectum* with major prolation); (2) the full circle without dot (*tempus perfectum* with minor prolation); (3) the half circle with dot (*tempus imperfectum* with major prolation); and (4) the half circle without dot (*tempus imperfectum* with minor prolation). To these usual signs we should add the figure 3, which occurs in four dances (*Giove, Ingrata, Pizoccara,* and *Prisoniera*).

Where parallel versions of the same tune exist, various discrepancies in the use of the mensural signs appear. Some of these do not, apparently, affect the actual rhythm of the music. Such is the case with *Ingrata*, in which Domenico uses a clear C3 for the sixth strain, while Giovanni and Guglielmo have the half circle with dot for the same music. The versions of *Giove* by Cornazano and Domenico use the sign C3, but here the C appears to be crossed with a diagonal or almost horizontal line (not like the vertical line of *tempus diminutum*, which vertical line appears nowhere in the dances). For exactly the same music of this strain Giovanni and Guglielmo have no sign. Again, the notation of the last strain of *Pizoccara* is clearly in major prolation. Domenico's choreography prescribes *piva* for this strain, and the scribe writes the music with a simple 3. The versions of Giovanni and Guglielmo have the same music with no sign, but the choreography is lacking in each.

At other times, the use of different signs in parallel versions produces different meters and rhythms in the music. Such is the case in *Prisoniera*. In Giovanni's choreography one section (the sixth strain of the music) is called *saltarello todesco*, and is clearly noted in major prolation, with the sign 3. Domenico's choreography calls for *piva* with this strain, and Guglielmo for *saltarello todescho*; but their music, alike in both cases, is a simple modification of Giovanni's melody transposed a fourth higher, and plainly written in minor prolation.

Where four parallel versions of the same tune are extant, the signs are sometimes in agreement in all of them, as in the third strain of *Belreguardo*, and the fifth strain of *Leoncello*, in which all four versions have a basse dance passage signed with the half circle and dot. This, however, is not always the case. In *Mercantia*, Guglielmo's scribe gives the basse dance of the third strain the full circle with dot, while the other three versions have the half circle with dot. The beginning of *Prisoniera*, with three versions, has an even greater variety: Giovanni Ambrosio has the full circle without dot, Domenico the half circle with dot, and Guglielmo the full circle with dot.

In actual notation, the *punctus divisionis* often appears wherever there are measures of six minims; but there, also, the usage of the scribes varies. There are many measures in which the division dot is used by one scribe and omitted by another. The *punctus additionis* or *augmentationis* is also used. In addition to this method of indicating dotted rhythm, it has also been deemed advisable, in passages in duple meter, to interpret the figure ♩ ♩ not as a triplet, but as ♩. ♩ (♩. ♪ in our transcription), a practice which became extremely common in the sixteenth century.

CLEFS AND KEY SIGNATURES

The clefs and the use of B-flat in the signature also require comment. The Brussels manuscript has a number of pieces without a clef, but Toulouze never omits it, nor do our Italian scribes, with the single exception of the Domenico version of *Marchesana*. In the latter, there is no clef throughout. The Giovanni version has the usual alto clef with B-flat, and Guglielmo has the alto clef without B-flat.

The clef used in almost all of the Italian *ballo* tunes is the C clef on the third line. In mensural manuscripts of the fourteenth and fifteenth centuries, the C clef was often made by writing a heavy letter "C." When the corners of this form are angular, it looks very much like the *podatus* of square plain-song notation, but in reverse, with the open side on the right. The early printers borrowed this reverse *podatus* form for their printed C clef, and it is also the form definitely used in our *ballo* notation. The F clef was also borrowed from square plain-song notation, but used three notes instead of two. Seated on the F line was a *virga*, with a downward stem on the right. Immediately following it were two of the rhombic or diamond forms used for the *punctum* in the combination neumes. The two diamonds embraced the F line, and are still preserved in the dots of our modern F clef. The printers often used, instead of the two *puncta*, two minims with diamond heads, one with an upward, and one with a downward stem. For a clef made with a reverse *podatus* followed by two diamond-headed minims vertically opposed, see Giovanni Ambrosio's version of *Belreguardo*. The four parallel versions of this dance offer quite a mixture of clefs.

The question of clef forms would have no place in our discussion, if some of the rare variants from the almost universal alto clef in reverse *podatus* form did not raise doubts as to their real meaning. Attention has been called (above, p. 9) to Guglielmo's recognition of two keys or scales, *B-quadro* and *B-molle*. He tells us that *B-quadro* is *molto più airoso* and that *B-molle* is *alquante più cruda e men dolce*. It seems almost as if Guglielmo were making some such distinction as is nowadays often made between major and minor. In fact, many of our *ballo* tunes do have a pronounced major or minor quality.

The alto clefs in our tunes are frequently accompanied by a B-flat as a key signature, but here, once again, the scribes do not always agree. In some of the tunes having parallel versions (*Belreguardo, Giove, Marchesana, Leoncello, Spero*) the flat appears in one version and is omitted in another. In other cases (*Figlia Guilielmino, Gelosia, Tesara*), where the melody cadences on B (flat), or on F, or where the tritone is disturbing, a B-flat seems absolutely necessary, even though it does not appear in the signature.

Another curious case is *Ligiadra*. We have two versions of the music: one in the Giovanni Ambrosio codex in Paris (*ital.* 476, fol. 65ʳ) and the other in the Paris Guglielmo Manuscript (*ital.* 973, fols. 51ʳ–51ᵛ). Both use the alto clef with B-flat. All strains in both versions up to the penultimate strain cadence on middle C, and do not go below this note, so that B-flat is not used. Up to this point the tune could be considered a pure C major. But the penultimate strain does run below C and cadences on B-flat. Having written this strain as described, the Giovanni Ambrosio version cancels it with the word "vacat," rewrites it to cadence on C, and then transposes the last strain a fifth higher, so that it also cadences on C, emphasizing the C major quality of the tune. The Guglielmo version writes the penultimate strain with a cadence on B-flat, like the canceled strain of the other version. Guglielmo's last strain is the same melody as Giovanni's, but it is written a fifth lower than Giovanni's and cadences on F, the only such cadence in the whole piece.

Since so many of our tunes do have a distinct major or minor quality, the few cases where the clef differs from the normal alto clef invite study. *Amoroso* is a case in point. It has a soprano clef and no flat, and reads very easily in this clef. The first and last strain end on D and the middle portion of the piece on A. The whole may well be in a

modal form of D minor, and the use of B-flat seems nowhere compulsory. *Voltate in ça Rosina* has a mezzo-soprano clef and no flat. It
reads in this clef like our modern A minor, and there seems to be no
reason for reading it otherwise. *Tesara* has a consistent tenor clef
throughout and no flat, and there are, unfortunately, no parallel versions
which might make possible a comparison, or which might confirm the
clef. The tune can be read in the tenor clef, but it then has a more
pronounced modal quality than the other *balli*. The author has transcribed the tenor clef reading, but is inclined to believe that the consistent tenor clef is an error for the alto clef with B-flat. *Verzeppe*
presents a similar tenor clef problem.

Belfiore, the music of which is given only in the Paris Domenico
codex, has a clef made with three notes on the third line, like a baritone
clef, but there is also a flat in the signature, in the second space from the
bottom. The piece begins and ends on the first line of the staff, which
would be B. If the flat in the original is really an E-flat, this note
would have to be B-flat. No other tune in our repertoire cadences or
runs as low as this, and the author has therefore transcribed it as if the
three-note clef were an error for the usual alto clef with B-flat. The
cadence note is then F and the piece makes a good F major.

The clef of *Sobria* is a puzzle, being like no other clef in our collection.
It is made with two signs, each like a very small *b-rotundum*, placed
vertically one over the other. In the two versions we have of this piece
(evidently copied from the same source: one is the Vatican Cornazano
codex, the other the Paris Domenico), these signs are differently placed.
Cornazano squeezes the two small flats, one above the other, into the
second and third spaces from the bottom, like the two notes of the
reversed *podatus*. It looks there as if an alto clef might be meant. In
Domenico, however, the two flats are placed in the first and third
spaces. This may be a scribal error, but the difference is carried through
on all the lines of the notation. Reading the strange clef as an alto clef,
the piece begins on F, and most of the strains cadence nicely on F or on
C. But, in the second strain of both versions, the last note is an additional and rhythmically anomalous white *longa* on E, and the piece
ends, in more normal rhythm, on another equally mysterious E.

ACCIDENTALS

Accidentals occur in the course of the notations, and are used very much as in the other mensural music of the period. The accidental sign, almost always a flat, is not always placed immediately before the note which it affects, but may precede it by one or two notes, as in *Gelosia*. In pieces having a B-flat in the signature and cadencing on B-flat or on G, the E-flat is not in the signature, nor is it introduced later in the piece, except in *Gelosia*, where it appears once as an accidental. In *Belreguardo*, *La Figlia Guilielmino*, *Colonnese*, and *Prisoniera*, the transcriber has not hesitated to add the E-flat over the staff. In *Tesara* the E-flat may be doubtful, as also the F-sharp over the staff in *Petit Vriens*.

A very interesting case is that of *Giove*. The notes of the four parallel versions are practically identical. Cornazano has no B-flat in the initial signature, but it appears as a signature in strain three. All the other versions have the B-flat in the beginning. In the course of this piece the E-flat is never indicated, but it is, none the less, compulsory; for scattered throughout the piece we find clear and indubitable accidentals for A-flat, D-flat, and even G-flat. These unusual flats appear in exactly the same places in all four versions, with the exception of one D-flat omitted by Cornazano in the fourth strain. The G-flat occurs in the cadence of strain four, making a Phrygian close on F.

In *Marchesana*, the versions of Domenico and Guglielmo (and not that of Giovanni Ambrosio) show a faint sharp sign before the note A in the fourth strain. It is made in the modern form, and may have been added in a later, though still early, hand. It can have no other purpose than to warn the player not to use A-flat at this point (the preceding note is B-flat).

MODERN RESTORATIONS

There have been several attempts at practical restorations of this material for modern dancers. One, by Otto Gombosi,[20] employs the

---

[20] About Dance and Dance Music in the Later Middle Ages," *Musical Quarterly*, XXVII (1941), 289–305.

dance *Giove* — the tune with the unusual flats just discussed. Gombosi's transcription has a key signature of one flat, and the music is transposed up a major sixth. This transposition has changed some of the tone relations in the first strain: to conform with the original, the F in this strain should be F-sharp. In any case, Gombosi's transcription is more strictly modernized than that presented here. Gombosi's basse dance measures are in double values (above, p. 14). The steps fit accurately, for the choreography of the original is reasonably clear, and the dance is not long.

A more elaborate attempt at restoration has been made by Mrs. Mabel Dolmetsch in her *Dances of Spain and Italy from 1400–1600*.[21] She approaches the problem chiefly from the choreographical side. Her first example is the basse dance *La Spagna*. Taking the well-known *La Spagna* tenor (with some alterations), she places it in the bass, and composes to it a free, florid upper voice, filling in the texture with three- or four-part harmony. To this she applies the exact steps of Domenico's *La Spagna* choreography. A second dance is the *bassa danza Venus*, ascribed to Lorenzo the Magnificent in the Magliabecchi codex of Guglielmo. No music for this dance has come down to us, so far as is now known; and, assuming that "Venus" is a French name and not Italian, Mrs. Dolmetsch sought an adaptable composition of French origin. She chose the French chanson *Venus tu ma pris*, as found in Petrucci's *Odhecaton*, which, she believed, could be made to fit Lorenzo's steps. The music is, however, very freely modified. Finally, we have a *ballo, Gioioso*, but Mrs. Dolmetsch uses neither the steps nor the music of Giovanni Ambrosio (this dance is discussed in the next and final part of this study).

ROSTIBULI GIOIOSO AND ROTI BOULLY JOYEULX

The most interesting item in our collection of *ballo* tunes, as we now see them, is a *ballo* which furnishes a hitherto unnoticed close parallel with one of the pieces in the French sources. In the musical appendix of the Giovanni Ambrosio codex (Paris, *ital*. 476, fol. 66ʳ) there is a tune entitled *Gioioso*. In the choreographical text of this manuscript

[21] London, 1954.

the title reads *Rostibuli gioioso* (fol. 37ʳ). This is the only Italian source that has music for the dance, although its choreographical description appears in other Italian manuscripts, as *Rostiboli, Gioioso,* or *Rotiboli gioioso*. In English we might call it "The Jolly Roast and Boiled." It is always ascribed to Domenico as its inventor.

The Brussels basse dance manuscript and the Toulouze incunabulum contain a few pieces in which the notation varies from the usual unbroken series of black breves. These dances have added passages in white notation of semibreves and minims, which look exactly like the Italian *ballo* notation.[22] One of these pieces (no. 55 in Brussels) is entitled *Roti boully ioyeulx en mes. de braban.* In Toulouze (no. 20) it is *Roti bolli ioieulx*. The French versions clearly intend the performance of the white notation to *saltarello* steps, followed (as both sources specifically mention in the instructions) by *la basse danse* (Brussels) or *la bace* (Toulouze). The melody of the *saltarello* is quite clearly the same as that of the basse dance, except that the latter is more skeletal in form. There are a few discrepancies between the two French sources, but these are probably due to scribal errors in either, or to faulty register in Toulouze. They have been indicated in square brackets in our musical appendix.

The relation between Giovanni's Italian version of *Gioioso* and the tune as found in the French sources is extremely close and highly instructive. Giovanni devotes two strains to the white notation of the original, and two to the black. His *botte* or strokes are clearly written out in groups of three semibreves. He does not, however, adhere strictly to the rule that in the basse dance the notes should be doubled in value. In the first strain of the white *saltarello* notation, the first two notes (semibreves) of the motive (which is repeated slightly later) receive six semibreves each in Giovanni's arrangement, while all the other white semibreves receive only three. When Giovanni comes to the French black breve notation for the basse dance part, he gives each black breve only three white semibreves. The last strain has, in the

[22] The only writer who appears to have paid close attention to these mixed French notations is Friedrich Blume, in *Studien zur Vorgeschichte der Orchestersuite* (Leipzig, 1925).

French sources, black breves relieved in two places by two white
semibreves. This is treated by Giovanni in major prolation, each black
breve and each pair of white semibreves receiving one six-part measure.

The clef relation between Giovanni and the French sources is also
interesting. Both Brussels and Toulouze use a tenor clef without B-flat
for the white notation, and the equivalent F-clef on the second line for
the black. The melody thus rests on D. Giovanni, placing his notes
on exactly the same positions on the staff, uses the alto clef with B-flat
in the prevailing Italian fashion. His piece cadences nicely on F, and
can be regarded as pure F major.

It is probably no rash assumption to consider this Italian rendition
of a French tune as the kind of treatment which Guglielmo, in his
theoretical part, expects the player to give to the foundation *tinore* of a
ballo as well as of a basse dance, the composition or selection of which
he regards as the first requisite for the invention of a dance (see above,
pp. 8–9).

THE COLKELBIE SOW

The fame of *Rostiboli* extended beyond the continent, cropping up as
far away as Scotland. There is a fifteenth-century poem in Scottish dia-
lect, known as "The Tale of the Colkelbie Sow," which is mentioned
and quoted in Miss Maragaret Deane-Smith's study of Toulouze, "A
Fifteenth Century Dancing Book." [23] This poem was first printed
by David Laing in his *Select Remains of Ancient Popular Poetry of
Scotland*,[24] and appeared again in a later edition of Laing by John
Small.[25] The poem begins by relating that Old Colkelbie sold his black
sow for three pennies, and then goes on to tell, in three parts, how each
of the three pennies was spent. The scene of the first part is Scotland,
that of the second is France, and the third again takes place in Scotland.
The poet seems to have had a lively interest in dancing, for in the course

[23] *Journal of the English Folk Dance and Song Society*, III (1937), 100–109.
The author also cites, incidentally, the flyleaves of a *Catholicon* (Venice, 1497),
now in Salisbury Cathedral, on which are entered a score of dances with music,
among them eight with names that appear in the French repertoire.

[24] Edinburgh, 1822.

[25] Edinburgh and London, 1875.

of the poem he mentions numerous dances that were in use in his time. Our interest is primarily in the first part, which contains a long passage satirizing peasants who try to perform the aristocratic dances. A few verses from this caricature, which is not entirely intelligible, will show how our dance is involved:

> A maister swynherd, Swanky,
> And his cousin, Copyn Cull,
>
> . . . .
>
> Led the dance and began
>
> . . . .
>
> And other sum in consate
> At leser drest to daunce
> Sum *Orfute*, sum *Orliance*
> Sum *Rusty Bully with a bek*
> And *Every note in utheris nek*.

Orliance might well be the Orleans of the French repertoire. "Bek" (beck) is an old designation for a brook; but it is not easy to imagine what a *Rusty Bully* had to do with a brook.

It is a far cry from Italy to Scotland. We have surely not yet reached the limits of what future research may reveal about the nature, the origin, and the actual practice of these fifteenth-century dances and their tunes. It is with the hope that they may stimulate further and more fruitful study that the tunes and the ideas here set forth are offered.

DISCUSSION

Panelists: Ernst Ferand, Erich Hertzmann, Gustave Reese

Professor Ferand: I should like to ask a very basic question, which has intrigued me for many years. I do not think I can make any contribution toward its solution, but I may, at least, bring it up. Briefly, which was first, the hen or the egg? The dance or the music? There seem to be only two references in contemporary sources which shed light on the relation of the choreography and the music. The first is mentioned in Dr. Kinkeldey's paper on Guglielmo Ebreo.[26] Guglielmo gives a few musical directions: since the music of the dance may be in either of two keys or scales — *B-molle* or *B-quadro* — the dancer must recognize whether a given tune is in one or the other. Also, the composer of a new piece of dance music should first determine whether it shall be in *B-quadro* or *B-molle*, and then call upon his fantasy to provide a fundamental melody (*tinore*). This latter should, in the case of the *ballo*, be lively.

The other reference is in the Giovanni Ambrosio codex. Giovanni Ambrosio describes, in a letter, how Ippolita Sforza had found a new French tune in Naples, and composed a *ballo* to this tune. There may be more references of this sort, but, if so, I am not aware of them. In the light of this evidence, was the music written first, and the choreography adapted to it, or vice versa? It would seem, also, that the *ballo* was more pantomimic in nature than the basse dance; and this, too, might influence the question.

I should like also to mention the intriguing question of the polyphonic elaborations of the basses dances, and perhaps also of the *balli*. It was, I believe, Dr. Hertzmann who first pointed out that the basse dance melodies were meant to be accompanied by improvised added parts.[27] The first notated polyphonic version that we know of is a two-voice setting of the *Spagna* melody preserved in Manuscript 431 of the Perugia Biblioteca Communale;[28] and there is a second one, not too much later (probably from the 1480's) found both in Petrucci's *Canti C*, and, intabulated for lute, in Spinaccino's *Libro Secondo*.[29]

These and other versions are considered by both Gombosi and by Bukofzer, but with varying results. Bukofzer felt that the two-voice Perugia setting was a written-out example of typical basse dance

---

[26] "A Jewish Dancing-Master of the Renaissance," p. 340. See also above, pp. 9 and 19.

[27] Erich Hertzmann, "Studien zur *Basse danse* im 15. Jahrhundert," *ZfMw*, XI (1928–29), 411.

[28] Fols. 95ᵛ–96ʳ (formerly 105ᵛ–106ʳ). Also Bologna, Liceo Musicale, MS 109, fols. 59ᵛ–60ʳ

[29] *Canti C*, 148; Spinaccino II, 31. The beginning of the *Canti C* version is given in Bukofzer, *Studies in Mediaeval and Renaissance Music* (New York, 1950), p. 205.

improvisation, but that such pieces as the Spinaccino version just mentioned were much too imitative to have been improvised.[30] Here I disagree not only with Bukofzer, but with all those scholars who, although they admit the importance of improvised music in general, and of improvisation in the basse dance in particular, feel that improvisation necessarily implies primitive and inartistic music. Willi Apel, for instance, in his article "A Remark about the Basse Danse"[31] mentions Kotter's versions of the *Spagna* as truly improvised music, simply because there are so many parallel fifths and octaves. I believe, however — and I have good witnesses for this belief — that improvisation in this period could be quite elaborate. Zarlino presents quite complex improvisational settings. Calvisius observes that there are many musicians who can improvise counterpoints and fugues.[32] Since this is difficult to do, he gives about twenty examples of how it might be done. The fact is, however, that it *was* done. In German theoretical literature of the period, such improvisation was known as "sortisatio"; and the obscure writer Joachim Thüring (Thuringus) observes, in the early part of the seventeenth century, that an example would be something like the *Stabat mater* of Josquin des Près. Now one could hardly imagine anything more complex contrapuntally than this piece, which has a *cantus firmus* in the middle voice, with imitative parts above and below. In the light of this, I see no reason why the various examples of polyphonic basse dance given by Bukofzer and Gombosi should not be patterns for improvised elaborations of the melody.

Professor Hertzmann: I should like to take back, now that I have the occasion, one of the points which I made in my article.[33] I ventured there, in my innocence, that the basse dance tunes were folk songs, or, to put it less strongly, popular tunes. I no longer believe this: I think, in fact, that everything speaks against such a theory. In the first place,

---

[30] *Studies,* pp. 200, 206.
[31] *Journal of Renaissance and Baroque Music,* I (1946), 140–141.
[32] In the last chapter of the *Melopoeia* (1592). Cf. K. Benndorf, "Sethus Calvisius als Musiktheoretiker," *VfMw,* X (1894), 449.
[33] "Studien zur *Basse danse* im 15. Jahrhundert," *ZfMw,* XI (1928–29), 401.

chansons that may have some folk connection (such as *L'homme armé*)
are not among those which served as sources for basse dance melodies.
Nor do we find any basse dance references in literature, in polytextual
songs, or in quodlibets. The only piece that might suggest popular
music is the chanson *Sur le pont d'Avignon*,[34] related to the basse dance
Avvignon; but I tried even twenty-eight years ago to establish relationships among the various versions of this piece, without success.

There is, I think, an even stronger reason why these basse dance
tunes were not popular songs. Both the basse dance and the *ballo* had
(in contrast to Gombosi's opinion) [35] *mesures*: a French basse dance
might have, say, forty notes, and anywhere from three to six *mesures*.
After each *mesure* there comes a *branle* (as we learn from the choreographic instructions), and then there is a new *mesure* with single
steps. These choreographic divisions never agree, as far as I can find
out, with the incises of the melody of the chanson used as the basse
dance tune: in other words, the versification of the chanson (when it is
known from non-dance settings) is in no way reflected in the dance
arrangement. But, if the source melody were a popular one, the basse
dance steps would have had to be tailored to fit it, in order that the
tune might have been sung (for, as the writers of the period tell us,
such tunes were also sung). Thus I do not believe that there is anything
popular about the basse dance tunes; nor do I believe that the tunes
fit the texts as they were sung. The choreography simply does not agree.

The tunes were, rather, abstractions. A good example is the tenor of
the Mass *La bassa danza* by Faugues,[36] which may well be a basse
dance no longer extant elsewhere. This tune of about forty notes (a
normal length for a basse dance) appears in long notes in the tenor of
the Mass, and the actual dance tune might easily be reconstructed —
abstracted, as it were — from it. In short, the basse dance tunes were,
indeed, melodies already known, but they were abstracted from their

[34] Found in two versions, one anonymous (*Canti C*, 62), and the other by
Claudin (in a manuscript appendix to some Attaingnant prints: Paris, Bibliothèque
Mazarine, 39 345 A). See Hertzmann, "Studien zur *Basse Danse*," p. 408.

[35] "About Dance and Dance Music in the Late Middle Ages," *MQ*, XXVII
(1941), 301–302.

[36] Trent Codices, nos. 1151–1155.

original sources, and completely distorted to fit the purposes of the choreography.

Professor Reese: Dr. Kinkeldey has pointed out[37] that there are only three basse dance melodies which have come down to us in the Italian repertoire, the other melodies being *balli*; and that, in the French repertoire, the reverse situation obtains: there are many basse dance melodies, and practically no *balli*. Since the *ballo* is made up out of components of the different kinds of basse dance, rearranged for the purpose of achieving individual choreography in each *ballo*, it would seem that the *ballo* represents a more advanced stage in the technique of the dance than does the basse dance. Thus, if a dancing master were preparing a manual, he would present the easier material — the basse dance — first. He would then go on to the *ballo*. I wonder, therefore, if certain conclusions in the literature on the basse dance may not be slightly risky. I refer especially to the conclusion that the Italians were more interested in "free expression" than the French[38] — that the French basse dance suffered from a sort of hardening of the arteries. This may be true, of course, but it is also possible that the French sources are simply concerned with earlier stages of the dance; and that their manuals are not as comprehensive or advanced as those of the Italians, which go beyond the basse dance to the *ballo*, and dwell on that.

Another question arises: what might the longevity of the basse dance influence have been? We all know that the basse dance and *saltarello* tended to die out with the rise of the pavan and galliard. Nevertheless, older artistic expressions have a way of lingering on: Monteverdi, after all, wrote a Mass based on a motet by Gombert. I wonder if the basse dance influence could have survived in any way (perhaps as something archaic) in connection with Monteverdi's *Ballo delle Ingrate*.

Dr. Kinkeldey: In regard to your first comment: the basse dance in France was much simpler and more stereotyped than in Italy. The Italian basse dance descriptions sometimes approach the complexity of

[37] Above, pp. 5, 8.
[38] See, for example, Gombosi, "About Dance and Dance Music," pp. 302–304.

the *balli,* even inserting into a basse dance, "here they make two measures of *saltarello,*" or, "here they make six measures of a *saltarello tedesco."* What you saw in *Roti boully* was actually a *saltarello,* followed by a real basse dance notated as such and based on the same melody.

PROBLEMS OF AUTHENTICITY IN EIGHTEENTH-CENTURY MUSIC

H. C. Robbins Landon

In the summer of 1951, Jens Peter Larsen, Ernst Fritz Schmid, and the writer held a miniature conference in Bad Aussee. The purpose of this meeting was to determine the authenticity and the chronological order of some one hundred divertimenti for chamber orchestra by Haydn. Each of us had notes on the sources, and on various eighteenth-century catalogues in which these divertimenti appeared. As the conference progressed, and we exchanged all our information, some kind of order began to appear in the utter chaos of these hundred odd works. A number appeared in catalogues and on manuscript sources under the names of other composers, such as Leopold Hof(f)-mann, Franz Aumonn (Regenschori at the monastery of St. Florian), Joseph Schmitt, Holzbauer, and so on. We had scores even of these spurious works, and in each case our external evidence was matched by equally convincing internal evidence; that is, the music contained harmonic, orchestral, and melodic details which were foreign to Haydn's style.

After we had thus combined all the external and internal evidence at our disposal, we were left with about sixty works which had survived, as it were, the initial ordeal of fire and water. Of these sixty, about forty were unquestionably genuine in that they were included in one or both of the authentic Haydn catalogues (the first of these is the so-called *Entwurf-Katalog*, a running draft which he kept from about 1765 to 1800, and the second the definitive *Haydn-Verzeichnis*, prepared by Haydn's valet and factotum, Johann Elssler, in 1805). A few works, such as the *Notturni* for the King of Naples, existed in autograph or authentic parts but were missing from the catalogues; naturally, such compositions raised no problems of genuineness.

The final stage of our investigations was undoubtedly the most difficult. It was our task to make decisions on a group of divertimenti which had come down to us in manuscript and printed sources bearing Haydn's name, but which were missing in the authentic catalogues, and for which there was no other real evidence of authenticity. In some cases, the sources were very late — as late as the beginning of the nineteenth century, and the works so impossible from the stylistic standpoint that we had no hesitation in dismissing them. Subsequently the writer has found the correct authors for many of these exiled works, and Hoboken's catalogue will probably reveal still more. But there was one A major work, among all these obvious forgeries and misattributions, which struck all three of us as being a typical Haydn symphony of the period 1761–1765. It exists under Haydn's name in two sources: a set of manuscript parts, dated 1766, in the Benedictine Monastery of Göttweig in Lower Austria; and in the so-called *Quartbuch*, a thematic catalogue of unknown origin which came into Haydn's hands in the 1790's. Göttweig contains one of the largest and most important Haydn collections in Austria, and there is strong evidence that both Joseph and his brother Michael had direct contact with the monastery, Michael as early as 1759 and Joseph a few years later: there are very few spurious Haydn works at Göttweig. As far as the *Quartbuch* is concerned, the situation is a little more complicated. There are a good many spurious Haydn symphonies in this catalogue; some are by Michael — the *Quartbuch* lists them simply as "Haydn" — and some by other composers. When Haydn was making up the symphonic list for his catalogue of 1805, he used the *Quartbuch* together with his own earlier *Entwurf-Katalog*, and in the process of sifting the authentic from the spurious works he crossed out several incipits in the *Quartbuch*.[1] The little A major symphony, however, was not crossed out.

From the standpoint of the external evidence thus far presented,

[1] Jens Peter Larsen, *Die Haydn-Überlieferung* (Copenhagen, 1939), pp. 248ff; concerning the Symphony, see also p. 269 ("Parthia" in A).

there is a fairly strong case for this symphony. And this external evidence is supported by considerable internal evidence. The work has that strong rhythmic drive, that forward push which is so characteristic of Haydn's symphonic music in the early 1760's. There are several other confirming details: for instance, the nervous bass line, with its repeated quarter notes; the lean orchestration, in which oboes and horns are sparingly but tellingly used; and so forth. In 1951, the one mark against it — and this was a fairly serious one — was the fact that Haydn omitted the symphony in the *Haydn-Verzeichnis* of 1805. Nevertheless, after we had analyzed the work and played it several times, we decided to include it in the *Gesamtausgabe*, although it was the only work which was to be accepted without positive evidence of its genuineness.

Some years later, when the writer was working in Sigmaringen Castle, he found the symphony again, in the Sigmaringen Catalogue of 1766; but not under Haydn. The work was listed among the compositions of one Carlos d'Ordoñez.[2]

Obviously the problem of this symphony could not be solved without undertaking a thorough study of Ordoñez. Space prohibits more than a summary here, but the writer hopes to present the material in full at some future occasion. Ordoñez — the name appears in various sources as Ordonnez, Ordonitz, and with a Germanicized version of his Christian name (i.e., Karl von) — seems to have been born in Vienna of Spanish parents; the name is not an uncommon one in Spain. The *Totenprotokollregister* of the City of Vienna lists his dates, 1734–1786, and old periodicals and musical dictionaries yielded a certain amount of supplementary information. He was a civil servant in the *Niederösterreichische Landrechten*, but as early as 1766, we find him mentioned in Hiller's *Wöchentliche Nachrichten* (Leipzig, 23 September, 1766, p. 99) under Viennese violinists as: "Herr Carl von Ordonitz, Registrant bey den Landrechten, in Sinfonien [bekannt]." Indeed, he seems to have been known even earlier, for some of his symphonies were auctioned in Stockholm in 1762, together with those of Hasse, the Grauns, Domenico dall'Oglio, Galuppi, Wich, Araya, and

[2] See Landon, *The Symphonies of Joseph Haydn* (London, 1955), pp. 24ff and p. 820 (no. 119).

Neruda.[3] Wurzbach's *Lexikon* suggests that he was a violinist in the Emperor's *Hofcapelle*; but his name is not found in Köchel's *Die Kaiserliche Hof-Musikkapelle in Wien von 1543–1867* (Vienna, 1869), nor would such a position have been compatible either with his aristocratic background or with his position as a civil servant. He did, however, participate in the concerts of the *Tonkünstler-Societät* during the 1770's. When in Vienna in 1772, Burney heard Haydn quartets at the English ambassador's house, played by Starzer, Ordoñez, Count Brühl, and Joseph Weigl.[4]

Ordoñez's music is scattered throughout the libraries of Austria, Germany, Italy, and France, and as far afield as England: the British Museum and Royal College of Music own manuscript copies of his string quartets. Not much was published: Guera of Lyon issued two sets of string quartets (a total of twelve) and a symphony or two; some cassations — which cannot be located — and two or three more symphonies were printed in Paris. The bulk of his *oeuvre* remains in manuscript. In various trips through central Europe, the writer has located some sixty symphonies, thirty string quartets, twenty string trios, and isolated other works, such as two operas (one of which, *Alceste*, was performed at Esterháza), a violin concerto, and so on. Three things emerged very clearly from this study: (1) Ordoñez was one of the most original and talented composers of his day; (2) the disputed Symphony in A Major is unquestionably by him; (3) this was not the only work of his to be erroneously attributed to Haydn.

As far as the first point is concerned, space does not permit the detailed analysis which the material requires. The writer has edited another symphony, in C major, scored for three choirs, two of trumpets and kettledrums and one of oboes, horns, strings, and organ; this work was played in a series of preclassical symphonies which the writer gave on the B.B.C. in 1956, and will be published shortly. Suffice to say that — apart from a Reutter work in manuscript parts in Heiligenkreuz Monastery — the whole structure of the work is unique, com-

---

[3] S. Walin, *Beiträge zur Geschichte der schwedischen Sinfonik* (Stockholm, 1941), p. 202.

[4] *Present State of Music in Germany* . . . (London, 1773), p. 290.

bining the Venetian multiple-choirs technique with the language of the
preclassical symphony. But apart from its historical interest, the work
is fascinating as music (we mention this piece in particular, because
it will soon be available for study). In future, no student of the eighteenth century can afford to overlook this talented and curious composer: the infusion of contrapuntal technique into the early classical
string quartet, hitherto studied almost exclusively through Haydn's
Opus 20, is also an important feature of Ordoñez's quartets.

The Symphony in A Major subsequently appeared in another manuscript source as Ordoñez: Jan LaRue located a set of parts in the Für-
stenberg Library at Donaueschingen. Apart from this confirmatory external evidence, however, there are many subtle details which — now
that we know — are quite typical of Ordoñez. May we limit ourselves
to one? Ordoñez almost invariably approaches a trill preceded by the
same note by means of an appoggiatura. This prevails whether the trill
is simply written ⟨music⟩ or with a *Nachschlag,* ⟨music⟩. A few characteristic examples are shown in Example 1.

A. Sinfonia in C for three instrumental choirs (manuscripts in Estense Library, Modena D. 289 and Florence Conservatory D.5.68)

B. Sinfonia in C (2 ob., 2 hns., 2 trpts., timp., str.; Modena D.603, Göttweig
Abbey, Sigmaringen Cat.)

C. Sinfonia in A (2 ob., 2 hns., str.; Modena E. 173)

D. Sinfonia in A for 2 ob., 2 hns., str., attributed to Haydn in Göttweig and
Quartbuch; to Ordoñez in Sigmaringen Cat. and Donaueschingen.

[continuation of bars 3–4 in sequence]

Just what he means by this appoggiatura is not clear, because a trill would normally begin on the upper note anyway; but in any case we find this combination of a grace note with a trill throughout his music, whereas we almost never find it in Haydn's. In 1951, Larsen and the writer were rather puzzled by these appoggiature in what we then took to be a Haydn symphony; but we came to the conclusion that the Göttweig monk who copied the manuscript [5] might have added them; there are similar cases in which local copyists added just such appoggiature to trills, particularly in early monastery sources.

The third point was perhaps the most rewarding, as far as Haydn research is concerned; for we have now located no less than seven works by Ordoñez hitherto known only under Haydn's name:

Symphony in A (discussed above).
Symphony in C (See Landon, *The Symphonies of Joseph Haydn*, London, 1955, p. 801).
Alceste, marionette opera (Landon, p. 861).
Divertimento (Notturno) in F (Larsen, *Drei Haydn Kataloge*, Anhang, III, F 9).
Divertimento (Concertino) in F (Larsen, III, F 12).
String Quartet in B-Flat (Larsen, IX, B 5: also appears under Vanhal's name).
String Trio in G (Larsen, V, G 5).

We have discussed the problems of this A major symphony in some detail, not to prove the fallibility of musicologists, but to show that internal, i.e., stylistic, evidence is a very subjective and — for the purpose of drawing any definite conclusions — a very limited criterion. It does not seem to matter how brilliant the critic is: when dealing with works of doubtful authenticity the stylistic element almost invariably leads to the wrong conclusion. A few concrete examples must suffice here. The so-called "Jena" Symphony, discovered by Fritz Stein in the music archives of the university town of Jena, was attributed to Beethoven on the following grounds: external evidence — the pres-

---

[5] It is signed by Pater Leander, who was, as we know from other sources, a "Magister Scholae Gottwicensis." See also Landon, article "Göttweig" in *Musik in Geschichte und Gegenwart*, V (1956), 461ff.

ence of Beethoven's name on two of the manuscript parts; internal evidence — a long list of comparisons with other early works by Beethoven. In fact, the symphony is by Friedrich Witt (1770–1837), and exists under that name in old parts at Göttweig. Moreover, if Stein had examined the external evidence more thoroughly, he would have arrived at Witt almost at once. The parts at Jena have watermarks which, as Stein wrote, otherwise appear in Jena only in an A major symphony by Witt. On the first violin part of the Jena MS., the copyist wrote the following set of initials: "P:F:W:". Stein reads the "F:W:" as Fritz Wegeler, Beethoven's friend and biographer. Of course they stand for Friedrich Witt.[6]

A second example concerns the mass of doubtful works found in the appendix — and occasionally in the main part — of the Köchel Catalogue. The Symphony or Overture in B-Flat Major, K^3 311a, was published by Adolf Sandberger. (Sandberger also "rediscovered" 78 Haydn symphonies, of which the real names for about 50 have been discovered.) It is quite fantastic that this impoverished overture, with its incredible blunders of part writing and orchestration, can have anything but a very remote connection with Mozart. Musicology should reverse the common law, and judge a doubtful work guilty until it is proved beyond doubt to be innocent. The curious thing about Mozart research is that serious investigation of these doubtful works has begun only comparatively recently. The *Neue Mozart Ausgabe* has appointed a brilliant scholar, Ernst Hess, to be sub-editor of the "Zweifelhafte Werke," and we may expect him to find the real authors for most of the "doubtful" compositions.

The gullibility of publishers and the musical public is apparently unlimited. A few years ago Schott published six "quartetti capricciosi" from manuscript parts in Czechoslovakia which bear Mozart's name. Despite the fact that Einstein, who knew the works, did not bother even to list the works under spurious compositions in the third edition of Köchel, both editor and publisher did not hesitate to print these six quartets. One example, from the first Quartet in A Major, will serve (Example 2).

[6] See Landon, "The *Jena* Symphony," *Music Review*, XVIII (1957), p. 109.

Example 2.

(The fugato here follows a slow introduction: a continuo part is obviously required.) In this case, one may be permitted to use internal evidence negatively; but Dr. Karl Pfannhauser has discovered the autographs and we may expect the results of his research in the near future.

Recently, when the writer was at Göttweig for another purpose entirely, he glanced through the Masses in the Göttweig thematic catalogue of 1830. This very cursory examination at once revealed the correct authors for two Mozart Masses found in the Köchel appendix: K[3] Anhang 233, a Mass for 4 voices, strings, 2 clarinets, 2 bassoons, 2 horns, and organ is listed as a work of Pichler; [7] while the Mass K[3]

[7] Constanze Mozart told the chorus director Jähndl in Salzburg that the work was by Franz Xaver Süssmayr, but Einstein lists no sources in the third edition of Köchel. In fact there exist at least two manuscripts under Süssmayr's name, one in the Royal College of Music, London (cat. 392), and one in Kremsmünster Monastery (see P. Altman Kellner, *Musikgeschichte des Stiftes Kremsmünster*,

Anhang 235$_c$ turns out to be the *Missa Solennis "Lotare filia Siona"* by Haydn's chapel organist at Eisenstadt, Franz Novotny (d. 25 August 1773: see Pohl, *Joseph Haydn*, I, 261). The Göttweig source is dated 1771. Having found these works quite by accident, the writer then looked at another thematic catalogue of which he has photographs, the Freising Catalogue. Freising was an important archbishopric in southern Germany and once owned a large collection of secular and sacred music; only the catalogue, now in the *Kreisarchiv* at Munich, has survived. On the second page, a third spurious Mozart Mass appeared. The work in question is a large-scale *Missa*, K[3] Anhang 233a, for 4 voices, strings, 2 oboes, 2 horns, 2 trumpets, kettledrums, and organ: in Freising it is catalogued under Johann Michael Dem(m)ler (d. 1784),[8] *Domorganist* at Augsburg (it was Demmler who played the first piano part of the Triple Concerto in F [K. 242] at a concert which Mozart gave at Augsburg on 22 October 1777; Mozart himself played the second solo part, and the pianoforte manufacturer Stein the third).

Of course what is urgently needed for every genre of music is the type of systematic locator catalogue inaugurated by Jan LaRue for eighteenth-century symphonies. Possibly the most important lacunae are string quartets and Masses; the writer has started a locator file for the string quartets, and perhaps we can persuade someone or some institution to undertake the Mass catalogue, which would be very large. Until we have cross-referenced files of this kind for all important categories of eighteenth-century compositions, research into the doubtful and spurious works of the masters will remain for too empirical.

In closing, we should like to add a few words on the subject of lost works. Fortunately both Mozart and Haydn kept systematic catalogues of their works, Haydn after about 1765 and Mozart from February 1784 to his death. Thus we know of a considerable number of lost works by both composers, which, if rediscovered, can be verified immediately by holograph *incipits*. Hitherto we have, by and large, searched

---

Kassel/Basel, 1956, p. 506). Whether Pichler or Süssmayr is the composer cannot be decided without further research.

[8] See Abert, *Mozart*, 7th ed. (Leipzig, 1955), vol. I, p. 452, n. 2.

for these lost works under Haydn's and Mozart's name. Recently the writer discovered — quite by accident — one of Haydn's lost Masses in Göttweig Abbey among the anonymous manuscripts. The circumstances surrounding the Mass and its rediscovery may prove useful to other scholars for similar purposes, and are herewith given in brief form.

Haydn lists fourteen Masses in his "Catalogue of all those compositions which I can approximately remember having written between my 18th and 73rd year" (*Haydn-Verzeichnis*). Two of these were believed to be lost: the *Missa Sunt bona mixta malis* in D minor, and a Mass in G. Both are also listed in the *Entwurf-Katalog*. The Mass in G appears on the left-hand margin of page 15 together with several others:

> Missa brevis in F.
>   a due Soprani
> Missa in Tempore Belli [1796]
> Missa Sti Ofridi [Missa Sti. Bernardi de Offida, 1796]
> Missa in Angustÿs. [Nelson Mass, 1798]
> Missa Rorate coeli desuper
>   in g.

When Haydn's valet and copyist, Johann Elssler, prepared the Masses for the *Haydn-Verzeichnis* he must have needed an enlarged *incipit*, which Haydn seems to have supplied from memory. As no. 5 of the Masses, Elssler lists the G major work, but without the title found in *Entwurf* (Example 3).

Example 3.

We may ask ourselves why Haydn includes what must be his two earliest extant Masses in the *Entwurf-Katalog* together with three very late works. The explanation is, we think, relatively simple. The *Entwurf-Katalog* was begun about 1765, and Elssler's father, Joseph (who died in 1782), started the catalogue off by putting down all those works of which Haydn still owned copies, or which he could clearly remember having written. Many of the very early period, however, from *c.* 1750 to 1760, are missing, probably because Haydn no longer had copies of them, and could not remember the *incipits.* In the course of the next thirty years, Haydn tried to keep the *Entwurf-Katalog* up to date, adding blocks of *incipits* every few years. When he returned from England, his attention turned to the Mass form, and he wrote the six great works of 1796–1802. During this late period, the very early *Missa brevis* in F, which he had long forgotten, was brought to his attention, and his biographer Dies reports Haydn's delight at the rediscovery. In this connection, the composer may have remembered another product of his early years, the G major Mass; and so it came about that these two, together with three late Masses, were entered in the *Entwurf-Katalog* sometime after the year 1798. Probably the entry may be dated in the year 1798 or early in 1799 — at any rate before he completed the next Mass, the so-called *Theresienmesse* of 1799.

On 7 March 1957, the writer located the theme of the Mass in G in the Göttweig thematic catalogue of 1830. The work is found on p. 107, vol. I, under "uncertain authors": "[No.] 25 Missa a 4 voc 2 Violinis/-et/Organo/ prod. 1779," followed by the theme in two staves. Many of the anonymous Masses listed on that page of the catalogue have long since disappeared; but this work survived the nineteenth century, the German confiscation of the monastery during World War II, and the ensuing evacuation of all the manuscripts, first to another monastery, then to Vienna, and finally back to Göttweig. The important fact was that the cover originally bore Haydn's name; it read: "[Ornament]/ Missa,/ à / Canto, Alto,/ Tenore, Basso,/ Violinis 2 $\underline{\underline{bus}}$/ Con/ Organo,/ Del Sig $\underline{re}$ Josepho Hayden./ F: G:". The words "Josepho Hayden" were later canceled, probably at the beginning of the nineteenth century, when this Mass was no longer generally known. For this reason, it was then placed under "uncertain authors." Subsequently, the reverse sheet of the title page, which had been missing, was located; it served as the back part of the cover, and listed fifteen performances of the Mass at Göttweig, from "5 April $\overline{779}$" to "13. Februarii. $\overline{786}$." The copyist, too, could be identified: he was Franz Graff (1716–1779), organist at Göttweig and a prolific composer in his own right; apparently the monastery bought or acquired the manuscript after Graff's death, for the first performance at Göttweig Abbey took place after Graff had died.

The theme of the Kyrie in the Göttweig version differs slightly from that of Elssler (Example 4).

Example 4.

This is doubtless because Haydn quoted the *incipit* from memory both in the *Entwurf-Katalog* and in the *Haydn-Verzeichnis,* some forty years after he had written the Mass. The appoggiature are simply written out in the Göttweig copy, and Haydn seems to have confused the end of the first bar of Example 3 with the beginning of the second of Example 4, i.e., the run starts from e″ instead of a″. Unfortunately Haydn's memory was none too good, and he could list the beginning of the *Missa brevis Sti. Joannis de Deo* in the *Entwurf-Katalog* as in Example 5a instead of in the form of the autograph (Example 5b); with the result that Elssler took the first to be another work entirely, and listed each as a separate work in the final catalogue of 1805.

Example 5.

The title found in the *Entwurf-Katalog,* "Rorate coeli desuper" (Isaiah xlv, 8: "Drop down, ye heavens, from above . . .") is taken from the Introit for the fourth Sunday in Advent, and indeed the theme of the soprano entry in the Kyrie is possibly based on part of the Gregorian melody (transposed into G) [9] shown in Example 6.

[9] See *Liber Usualis,* p. 353; also H. Besseler, *Musik des Mittelalters und der Renaissance* (Potsdam, 1931), p. 59.

Example 6.

a - pe - ri - a [-tur]

Each of the Göttweig parts bears the rather obscure title: "Alla Capella" ("for the chapel" or "for the band": cap[p]ella can mean both). Stylistically the work may be dated about 1750, though in many respects it would seem to have been written before the early *Missa brevis* in F. Having scored the work, the writer soon encountered the most complicated editorial problems: apart from consecutive fifths and octaves, there were whole bars which required alteration. Some of these mistakes were copyists' errors, but some were obviously the fault of the young and inexperienced composer. The reader may examine these problematical passages by consulting the full score, which has recently been published by the Haydn-Mozart Press, London (Universal Edition). Although the other early Mass contains its share of "unlearned" part writing, it is by far more fluently written than the rediscovered G major work.

As the score went to press, the writer learned that this Mass also exists in various sources under the name of Haydn's teacher, Karl Georg Reutter, Jr. (1708–1772), the *Domkapellmeister* of St. Stephen's Cathedral in Vienna. In fact, a very early reference to the work is found in the music catalogue of Herzogenburg Monastery, lower Austria (most of the music therein listed no longer exists). The principal part of this catalogue, which was prepared in two copies (both are still extant), was compiled in 1751. The title of what would appear to be the original volume is as follows: "Catalogus / Selectiorum musicalium/ Chori Ducumburgensis [Latin name for Herzogenburg]/ quibus accedunt/ Instrumenta musica/ Diarium cantus Figuralis/ aliarumque functionum Musicae/ totius Anni/ Index generalis Catalogi/ conscripti Anno 1751." There are two types of Masses listed: "Missae Solemnes/ cum clarinis & Tympanis:" and "Missae: sine clarinis & Tymp:". As No. 121 of the latter category, we find our Mass listed as "Missa & Deus erat/ Verbum/ a 4 voc: Conc$\underline{\underline{tis}}$/ 2 violini e / organo/ Del Sig[nore] Reütter", followed by the first one and one-half bars of the organ part.

The work was entered after the original section of the catalogue had been completed, and it is difficult to date the entry exactly, but one would estimate that the group around No. 121 was added during the years 1751 to 1765. Haydn's own *Missa brevis* in F appears a few pages later.

Apart from this early catalogue reference, the late P. Norbert Hofer's manuscript *Thematisches Verzeichnis der Werke von Georg Reutter jun.* (Vienna, 1947; copy in the Austrian National Library, S.m. 28992), lists, on page 11, two sets of manuscript parts under Reutter's name: in Schlierbach Abbey (upper Austria) and in St. Paul Abbey (Carinthia). These manuscripts were unfortunately unavailable for comparison.

As far as the Herzogenburg Catalogue is concerned, one curious point should be noted: Herzogenburg has several thematic catalogues, including a rather small one in oblong format, written toward the end of the eighteenth century and comprising two volumes. In the first of these, which consists of Masses, we find the G major Mass again listed under Reutter's name (entry 44, *incipit* this time in the G-clef); but we also find Haydn's *Missa brevis* in F among a series of Masses by the *Regenschori* of St. Florian Monastery, Franz Aumon (or Aumann, 1728–1797), as entry 152 ("Missa in F. . .Del Sig: Aumann"). In the course of the last five years, the writer has been compiling a thematic catalogue of Aumon's music, and it is a curious fact that almost half of his known instrumental works have been, at some time or other, attributed to Haydn; thus, the misattribution of the F major Mass in Herzogenburg is not so simple as would first appear.

During the summer of 1957, the writer visited the monasteries of Lambach, Kremsmünster, Schlägl, and Melk in the hopes of being able to find further information about this puzzling (and it must be admitted rather disturbing) problem of the *Missa "Rorate coeli desuper."* His efforts were not unrewarded, but the results of his findings only added to the confusion; for, in the famous Lambach Catalogue of 1768 (for the title, *see* Landon, *The Symphonies of Joseph Haydn,* p. 609), the Mass is listed neither under Haydn nor under Reutter, but under the name of Franz Paul Ferdinand Arbesser (1719–1774), *Hoforganist* at Vienna. The entry in the Lambach Catalogue is on page 61, and was

added by another hand at a date somewhat later than that of the main
body of the manuscript:

Missae breves		
in G		
[*incipit* of organ	à 4 Voci	Arbesser
part, one bar]	2 Violini	
Kyrie	Organo é	
	Violone	

The authenticity of the Mass is thus disputed, to say the least. The
question whether it is by Reutter, Arbesser, or the young Haydn is indeed very involved, and a full discussion of the various problems requires far more space than is at present available. The following points,
however, should be noted:

1. The fact of Haydn's holograph entry in the *Entwurf-Katalog*. It
is unlikely that Haydn mistook one of Reutter's or Arbesser's Masses
for his own, for, particularly at the period when he entered the *incipit*
(about 1799: see above), he was very conscious of the Mass form. "Auf
meine Messen bin ich etwas stolz" is the remark on the subject which
the modest composer made to his biographer Griesinger. If this work
is not genuine, it is the only one in the whole *Entwurf-Katalog* (not
the *Haydn-Verzeichnis!*) on which any doubt can be cast.

2. The rather primitive, "schoolboy-ish" choral texture of this Mass
makes it impossible to believe that the mature Reutter, careful craftsman that he was, could have written it. The frequent consecutive fifths
and octaves, which are also, with very few exceptions, duplicated in the
Reutter sources enumerated above, point to a young and inexperienced
composer, not to the man who was in 1750 Vienna's foremost composer
in the field of church music. In this connection, the writer would point
out that several of Reutter's Masses seem to be falsely attributed to
him; and a thorough investigation of Reutter's Masses must of neces-
sity be preceded by a scrupulous examination of all the contemporary
Masses preserved in the Austrian collections. The writer noticed three
other works which exist under Reutter's name but which are almost
certainly by minor Austrian composers of that period.

To sum up, we suggest that, until conclusive evidence to the contrary is unearthed, this work may be regarded as Haydn's first Mass, preceding the *Missa brevis* in F by some years; possibly it may be his earliest preserved composition altogether. Doubtless Reutter suffered that which Haydn had to combat throughout his life: Viennese copyists, wanting to sell the Mass to the outlying monasteries and churches, substituted Reutter's name for that of the young and then completely unknown student; the same thing, of course, happened conversely to Haydn as soon as he became famous. Naturally, the writer will welcome any information which sheds light on this complex and curious problem, which has turned out to be one of the most baffling facing the Haydn scholar.

The fact that a lost Haydn Mass could be found among "Incogniti" at Göttweig Abbey suggests that we may find other lost works under anonymous manuscripts in European libraries. If the Austrian National Library can catalogue Mozart's *Schauspieldirektor* under "Incerti," it is by no means impossible that we may, one day, find Bach's *Marcuspassion* in an obscure East German church, or Schubert's "Gastein" Symphony somewhere in an uncatalogued Upper Austrian *Konzertverein*.

DISCUSSION

Panelists: Edward O. Downes, Karl Geiringer, Jan LaRue, Oliver Strunk

Dr. Sachs: I should like to step for a moment out of the role of chairman to mention these "appoggiatura trills." [10] In such a case, there is, of course, no true appoggiatura at all. Instead, the composer is specifying, by means of a note resembling an appoggiatura, whether the upper note is to be a whole tone above the principal, or a half tone. Thus, if the composer wants E-flat as an upper auxiliary, he writes the E-flat as an "appoggiatura," but this note is, of course, played as part of the trill. There is some explanation of this in, among others, Quantz. [11]

[10] Discussed in connection with the Ordoñez symphony; above, pp. 35–36.
[11] *Versuch einer Anweisung die Flöte traversiere zu spielen* (Berlin, 1752, etc.), IX, 9.

Dr. Landon: This still would not explain such cases as the Ordoñez Symphony in C for three choirs which I mentioned before.[12] There the trills are on C, and there could be no question of playing anything but D as the upper auxiliary. I have really been unable to think of any satisfying explanation for this habit. Perhaps Ordoñez wanted to be sure that the players would begin their trill on the upper note, in case they were tempted (having just played C) to begin it on the principal. This, however, would contradict C. P. E. Bach, Leopold Mozart, and others, who insist that the trill must always begin with the upper note, except in a few special cases.

Professor Ferand: May I contribute a bit of information? In the Bologna Liceo Musicale I found a source which is almost completely unknown: a treatise on ornamentation by Filippo Maria Gherardeschi [13] who was, I think, a pupil of Martini. This contains considerable information on this unusual trill, and would, I think, be worth following up.

Mr. Downes: There is one detail which I should like to mention while I have it in mind. I know of at least one symphony by Johann Christian Bach which has different incipits in two different versions: in one version, the first four measures simply do not appear. I do not know how often this happens, nor exactly what its effect would be on locator catalogues. . . .

Dr. Landon: That is exactly what happened with the "Jena" Symphony: it was for that reason that the Göttweig version was not discovered sooner. In the Göttweig variant, the symphony begins with a rousing unison accord on C, while the Jena version omits this. Mr. LaRue would have found it long ago in his locator catalogue, had it not been for this discrepancy.

Mr. Downes: Moreover, the incipits of first movements of so many eighteenth-century symphonies are extremely similar. There are also

---

[12] Above, p. 34.
[13] Presumably *Elementi per il cembalo*. See the article on Gherardeschi by Luigi Tagliavini, in *MGG*, V, cols. 57–58.

symphonies which, in different versions, have different middle movements. This may make a good deal of difference in dating a composition. And, of course, there is the old problem of identifying symphonies as opera overtures.

I should like to say that I agree very strongly with Mr. Landon about the use of stylistic evidence to decide the authenticity of compositions. In trying to authenticate certain works of Christian Bach, I made a collection of stylistic and formal traits which were supposed to be specifically his. One formal characteristic, for example, was a form of *da capo* aria approaching very closely to the sonata-allegro form, which Hermann Abert (who was, after all, a very distinguished scholar) considered to be an invention of Christian Bach.[14] Not only did I find that this form was cultivated by many other eighteenth-century composers prior to Christian Bach, but also that it could be traced back into the baroque, there being at least one example in Monteverdi. There is also a very striking stylistic trait, of beginning an aria with a very long sustained note, usually a dominant, which Einstein associates very closely with Christian Bach, as something which he had passed on to Mozart, and which he had derived from the capabilities of the *castrato* Manzuoli, who was popular in London just at the time when Mozart was working there.[15] In fact, of course, such a beginning may be found in many eighteenth-century arias. I have seen it in one published aria for Farinelli, and it would seem that many other singers of the period used the device. And, once again, if we go back to Monteverdi, we find it in the parody aria of Iro, beginning "Oh dolor," [16] in which the initial "Oh" is held for some eight measures. This appears to be a parody of a serious opera style better known at that time than we now realize. I offer these two examples as extreme illustrations of your caution about accepting internal evidence. Of course, as we learn more about the music, the risks will diminish; but, at the present,

[14] Hermann Abert, *W. A. Mozart* (appeared as the fifth edition of Otto Jahn's *Mozart*; 2 vols., Leipzig, 1919–21), I, 242.

[15] Alfred Einstein, *Mozart, sein Charakter, sein Werk* (English Edition, New York, 1945), pp. 356–359.

[16] At the beginning of Act III of *Il ritorno d'Ulisse* (Monteverdi, *Tutte le opere*, XII, 170).

nobody really knows enough about individual styles — certainly in the field of eighteenth-century opera — to be able to authenticate a piece on stylistic grounds alone.

I should like to put in a plea for being a little more charitable in your principle of assuming a work guilty until it is proved innocent: [17] there have been so many pieces for which we have originally had but slight evidence, and which have finally turned out to be genuine after all. I suggest that we put into operation a system like that used by Military Intelligence in the last war, according to which a report was judged both according to the reputation of its source, and according to the credibility of its facts compared with other evidence. A rating of A–3, for example, would represent a report from a usually unimpeachable source, which was not, however, clearly confirmed by other evidence. In the same way, we should balance the external and the internal evidence, and arrive at an accurate evaluation in that way.

Dr. Landon: I agree entirely with what you say. I was merely being "hard" because so many people have been so "soft." Anyone finding so much as a "B" on a manuscript has, in the past, so often assumed that the work was by Beethoven. And, naturally, it has been in the interests of publishers and performers to present a new work under a famous name, rather than some such unknown as Friedrich Witt. This is understandable enough, but it is a terrible fallacy all the same. For, now that we know that the "Jena" Symphony is by Friedrich Witt, we shall never hear it again: it is finished.

Dr. Smith: May I point out something? In 1932 I showed that a composition attributed to Haydn was spurious, being actually the work of Leopold Hoffmann.[18] The piece has since been published twice; and, although the publishers must know that it is by Hoffmann, they publish it as Haydn all the same.

---

[17] Above, p. 37.

[18] Carleton Sprague Smith, "Haydn's Chamber Music and the Flute," *MQ*, XIX (1933), p. 454, where the incipit of this *Concerto à Flauto Traverso* (D major) is given.

Dr. Landon: And it has been recorded four times, as well. At least two of the people who recorded it knew that it was by Leopold Hoffmann.

Professor Geiringer: You have clearly pointed out, and Mr. Downes has agreed, that it is dangerous to follow stylistic evidence in ascertaining the authenticity of a composition. I think we will all agree that the works of the young Haydn are very similar to those of other composers, and by no means always superior in quality. In such cases the stylistic evidence is, as you have observed, of no value.

You have also adduced examples to show that the evidence from manuscripts and libraries is also not wholly reliable. You mentioned a Mass of Haydn listed as "Uncertain" at Göttweig,[19] with the name Haydn crossed out. Then you gave us the example of the A major symphony which was attributed to Haydn in one library, and to Ordoñez in two others;[20] and, lastly, the "Jena" Symphony, which is at least partly attributed to Beethoven at Jena, and to Friedrich Witt at Göttweig.

My question is this: have you found in your researches any further sources which we *can* trust? When I began working on Haydn, many years ago, I learned my ABC's, so to speak, from Mandyczewsky, among others. I was told that the things to trust were the autographs, the Haydn catalogues (the Haydn-Elssler Catalogue, and the *Entwurf-Katalog*), the authentic prints made during Haydn's lifetime, either under his supervision, or at least with his full knowledge, and perhaps some good copies by Elssler or other completely reliable copyists. Can we add anything to this list? I am personally very much concerned with this question, as I have struggled with the problem of the authenticity of certain works which might or might not be Haydn, and which I should like to put definitely to the right or to the left.

Dr. Landon: I am afraid that I must shatter one more illusion: that of the infallibility of the Haydn-Elssler Catalogue. There is, in it, a list of *Divertimenti auf verschiedene Instrumenten*. Elssler compiled this list principally by using the *Entwurf-Katalog*; but apparently he also

---

[19] Above, pp. 40–41.
[20] Above, pp. 32–33.

used the *Quartbuch* and other sources, because there are some which are neither in the *Entwurf-Katalog* nor in any autograph which we know. Most of these are listed with a note as to the number of parts (*divertimento à 6*, and the like); but two are listed without any description whatever. It has turned out that these latter are not by Haydn, but by Johann Vanhal.[21] Mr. Larsen found one in the *Quartbuch*, and I found the second in Schwerin. Both were ascribed to Vanhal.

This, of course, raises a grim question: if such a mistake appeared in this case in the Haydn-Elssler Catalogue, does it occur elsewhere as well? We cannot be sure, of course, but I am inclined to think not. I believe that Haydn took great pains to sift out nonauthentic works when he compiled the catalogue, and that he often could be quite sure that a work was not his, even though he no longer remembered who had written it.

As for your reference to the Göttweig Mass,[22] I should like to mention a peculiar circumstance connected with it. I had sent a copy of the Mass we found to Leopold Nowak at the Österreichische Nazionalbibliothek, and he informed me that he thought he had discovered the autograph — in Rumania. Someone in the Austrian Ministry had written to Nowak in 1951, saying that there was in Rumania a Haydn autograph, dated 1756, and entitled *Missa Coelensis* (not the *Mariazeller* Mass,[23] but another piece). I was convinced, however, that 1756 was far too late for the Mass we had found, which is perhaps from 1750 or even earlier: it is one of Haydn's earliest works, full of incredible fifths and octaves in the part-writing. Moreover, the 1756 Mass is certainly not the other lost Mass in the Haydn Catalogue, which is entitled *Missa Sunt bona mixta malis*. Therefore the Rumanian autograph must be still a third Mass, hitherto unknown.

There can, of course, be little question of its authenticity, for it is an autograph. But, suppose that we had not known the autograph, and we had found a copy in some Viennese church. We should then have

---

[21] Also known as Wanhal, Van Hal, and Wanhall (1739–1813). The form of the name given in the text is apparently the original one.

[22] Above, p. 50.

[23] Also known as the *Missa Coelensis*.

been forced to rely wholly on internal evidence — a very nearly hopeless problem. It is true that if we are very careful, we may end up by leaving out of the Complete Edition some doubtful works which are really Haydn; but I think that it is far better to leave out a few doubtful early works than merely to assume that they are Haydn without adequate proof — in which case we shall have over a hundred *divertimenti* of which sixty are doubtful, very doubtful, or wholly spurious.

Professor LaRue: I should like to observe that we need to go quite a bit farther than locator catalogues, particularly in the realm of watermarks. We need watermark catalogues, and perhaps also handwriting catalogues. Do you not feel that there are some hands which recur so frequently that one could learn a good deal by having a list of them?

Dr. Landon: Yes, that is an essential point. Apart from the Elsslers and the other people from the Esterhazy Archives (who, curiously, never seem to turn up anywhere else), there are some copyists whom Haydn apparently used when he was in Vienna. After working with them for about ten years, I am gradually getting an intuitive feeling about them: such-and-such a copyist is very reliable; he makes fewer mistakes than the others, and so on. Thus, if we find a work of Haydn (assuming that there is no other evidence) in the hand of one of these more reliable copyists, that constitutes a point in its favor.

It is, however, the watermark and the paper which are essential. When we finally get together all the dated evidence in these areas, we shall be able to tell much more about the origin and date of an undated work than we can now. There are, for instance, certain watermarks which Mr. LaRue and I have studied which give clear indications of date. There is an Italian mark ("B V M" with an ornament over it) which is quite definitely late: 1790 or 1800. We can say, fairly certainly, I think, that it would never occur in a manuscript of the 1760's. Conversely, there is an "A S" watermark which occurs generally in the 1760's and 1770's, and possibly in the early 1780's. I have never seen this in a manuscript which we know was written in the 1790's or the 1800's.

Professor LaRue: I find the reaction generally among musicologists working in other periods that the application of watermark evidence in the eighteenth century is nonsense. The point that they make is: how can you tell who wrote on the paper, and when? What we are looking for with watermarks, however, is not exact information, but clues, which may eventually lead us into channels where exact information can be had. Would you agree with this?

Dr. Landon: Precisely. One can say to oneself, on the basis of watermark evidence: the evidence points to a date of 1760 or 1765, but not 1790 or 1800.

Professor Strunk: Let me say, first of all, that I sit here under false pretenses. I retired so many years ago from the field of Haydn specialization that I now feel like a fish out of water. I have done nothing with the subject for about thirty years, and I have never worked with it in European libraries, except for a day or so here and there. One reason that I can stay out of the subject with a clear conscience is that I see it now in such competent hands — Mr. Landon's and Mr. Larsen's.

Mr. Landon has made a very strong plea for the use of the external evidence in these questions, and has played down, in order to bring that out, the value of the internal evidence. Now it would seem to me that if the study of the internal evidence almost invariably leads us to the wrong conclusions, something is wrong with our methods. It puts us in the position of the man who says, "I smoke only Camel cigarettes," but who cannot tell a Camel from a Chesterfield unless he looks at the brand on the package. Let us look at the cases that Mr. Landon mentioned: for example, the Ordoñez Symphony in A Major.[24] Evidently a mistake was made here by Mr. Landon and Mr. Larsen, and I take it that the reason for the mistake was that this piece belongs to the early 1760's, a time that is difficult to work with using stylistic criteria. The style is very conventional, and the composers who are writing in it are quite young. The internal evidence is, I think, least valuable, when one tries to use it in the conventional stage of the development of a style, before real technical virtuosity and well-defined

[24] Above, pp. 32–36.

technical manners have developed. It is unreliable, too, when you work with the very beginning of a composer's career.

What about the "Jena" Symphony? Mr. Stein made a mistake here, and I think I would lay that mistake to what the Germans call "Entdeckerfreude." The work really took in nobody, so far as I can see. I don't recall a single writer on Beethoven who was ever convinced that Mr. Stein was right: even Riemann hesitated to commit himself, as I recall. Among the various people that I have talked with on the subject of the "Jena" Symphony over the last ten years, I could find no one who believed that it was by Beethoven. For all that, the work is not a bad one at all. One can date it: it is evidently quite late. Nevertheless, it makes no sense in the Beethoven framework; and, although there are many things in it which support the conclusion: Beethoven; there are many more which support the conclusion: not Beethoven.

Köchel 311a [25] took in Tiersot, and it took in Saint-Foix — a man of really infinite taste, but also a man who was something of a dilettante in such questions. That it really fooled Einstein I do not believe. He admits it into the main body of the Köchel Catalogue, but says, "mit allen Vorbehalten," and points out so many difficulties with the work that one can see that, although there was much evidence that seemed to point in the direction of Mozart, he wanted to resist it if he could.[26] The same thing would apply to the *Quartetti Capricciosi*,[27] and to the spurious Masses. The way in which Mr. Landon proposes to deal with these questioned works is, of course, the best one. There is nothing more satisfactory than to assign them to the man who actually wrote them: that ends the whole argument. But it is a very expensive way of doing it. It costs a lot of money; it costs a lot of time; and it costs a lot of effort. And, one wonders sometimes if the most spectacular results it achieves — as in the case of the "Jena" Symphony — are really worth it.

Now, on the other side: we have to use internal evidence anyway — not only with the questioned works, but also with the works that are

---

[25] The Overture (Symphony) in B-flat referred to above, p. 37.
[26] Einstein, *Köchel-Verzeichnis* (Leipzig, 1937), pp. 392–393.
[27] Above, p. 37.

not questioned, whenever the problem of date arises. Take the case of Mandyczewsky, who set up for himself criteria that practically prevented him from admitting any spurious works into the Haydn symphony canon. Still, he wished to establish a chronological order of the symphonies on the basis of external evidence alone; and, as we all know, this chronological order of Mandyczewsky[28] is very poor — sometimes because of mistakes, sometimes because he did not use all the external evidence, but often because he could not get a chronological order on the basis of external evidence alone.

A fine instance of what happens with external evidence was suggested to me the other day by Mr. Hertzmann: the Bach *Lukaspassion*. This is a work that is unquestionably in Bach's autograph. The watermarks are of no help, and the paper is absolutely correct: it is a Bach autograph from the 1730's. There is only one thing peculiar about the external evidence: it does not say on the title page that it is by Bach, and I gather from Mr. Mendel that this would be a rather unusual thing in a Bach autograph. The internal evidence, however, will not fit at all. Not only is it inconceivable that Bach could have written it in the 1730's, but it is also hard to believe that he could have written it at any time. Spitta thought that if one pushed it far enough back, it would be all right.[29] I take it that this was not *Entdeckerfreude*, but the desire to get rid of lost works of Bach, and to bring everything into a neat pattern.

We have many other illustrations of this kind: almost every composer has written out in his own hand, on his own music paper, compositions by other people. Mr. Hertzmann told me just the other day of a curious case he had heard of recently in Italy: madrigals by Verdi — real Verdi autographs. It turns out, of course, that they are simply copies of madrigals by Palestrina. It seems that one has to use both methods, external and internal, without relying wholly on either one.

One other thing that occurred to me in listening to the paper this morning is the role of system and accident. The systematic way to set to work is, of course, to make these locator catalogues; to have thematic

---

[28] As given in the list in the Haydn *Werke*, ser. I, vol. I, pp. iv–v.
[29] Philipp Spitta, *Johann Sebastian Bach* (2 vols., Leipzig, 1873–80), II, 338–339.

indices that are as complete as possible, and to have some system of classification so that one can find any given work. Still, many of the answers turn up by the merest chance, as in the case of the lost Haydn Mass: [30] Mr. Landon tells us that he was looking for something entirely different, and the Haydn Mass turned up purely by accident. We have all had that experience — that it is precisely when you are looking for something else that you find out the most interesting things. When you look for a needle in a haystack, perhaps you may turn it up by system, but often you find it simply by kicking the straws around.

[30] Above, p. 40.

INSTRUMENTAL MUSIC OUTSIDE THE
PALE OF CLASSICISM AND ROMANTICISM

Eric Werner

The development of instrumental music between and outside the classic and romantic schools has long been a stepchild of musical research. If it is not too easy to define clearly either the classic or the romantic persuasion, it is all but impossible to categorize those composers who swore allegiance to neither school. Hence they suffer the fate of many a nonconformist artist: the Procrustean bed of musicology, which is always ready for such problem children. Right at the outset of these observations I propose to use the terms "classic" and "romantic" only as rough semantic approximations, or if I may use the term, as dialectic conveniences. Instead I suggest a more "geo-musical" approach: it seems preferable to refer to a Vienna school (Haydn, Mozart, Beethoven, Schubert) and to a Berlin-Leipzig-Paris axis (Hoffmann, Weber, Chopin, Berlioz, Schumann). There are our two poles — and we shall now explore the instrumental music between them.

Unlike other periods of musical history, the one we shall consider moves on two distinct levels. On one level we distinguish between the mere craftsman and the artist; and on a second, no less important level, between the naïve and the reflecting composer. We must caution ourselves against identifying a priori the naïve composer with the mere craftsman, or the reflecting one with the artist. No: these levels frequently overlap. This strange fact was for the first time recognized and formulated by Schiller in his great essay about "Naive und sentimentalische Dichtung." There he says:

The opposite of naïve emotion is reflecting reason, and the sentimental mood is nothing but the result of the intention to reconstruct the naïve emotion under the aegis of reason. This might accomplish the ideal situation, wherein art meets nature again. . . .

The overwhelming majority of the musicians of our group between the classic and romantic poles consisted of naïve composers in Schiller's sense: and most of them were only advanced artisans.

This was felt by as late an observer as Schumann, who wrote: "There are many people without talent, who have learned a lot — they are the artisans."[1] This slightly unfair dictum indicates, none the less, the growing awareness of the divergence in position of artist and artisan as it arose at the turn of the eighteenth century.

The generation under consideration flourished between 1790 and 1830. Two revolutions actually determined its thinking and social position: 1789 and 1848. Geographically, most of our composers came from Germany, Central Europe, and Italy. France is hardly represented, England not at all. And yet, it was Paris and London which attracted and absorbed almost all of them. We refer to the following musicians:

Abbé Vogler	J. B. Cramer
Gossec	Viotti
Clementi	Hummel
Pleyel	L. Berger
Dussek	Moscheles
Cherubini	Reicha
Méhul	Mendelssohn

With the exception of Abbé Vogler, Hummel, and Berger, our composers spent most of their active lives in Paris or London. Why not in Vienna? This innocent question opens actually the gates to the problematic position of this little-known group. Vienna had become, after the death of Schubert, a stock exchange of "classic tradition" in instrumental music, and a branch office of the Italian export in opera. The romantics were at home in Berlin, in Paris, London, and later in Weimar, Dresden, and Leipzig. Our company, however, was by no

[1] *Gesammelte Schriften über Musik und Musiker* (Leipzig, 1888?), I, 30.

means slavishly dedicated to the classics, although some, like Pleyel, Hummel, or Moscheles, were disciples of Haydn, Mozart, and Beethoven, respectively. Vienna had lost its creative position for instrumental music — it was opposed to romanticism, and the aristocratic magnates, formerly the patrons (not too generous ones, by the way) of the classics, had lost much money after the Vienna Congress, and also their interest in instrumental music. Again they turned, probably for reasons of cultural policy, to Italian opera: let us not forget that Austria ruled over Lombardy and Venetia; that Hapsburg princes sat in Parma, Modena, Tuscany, and Naples. The old story happened once more: the politically conquered Italians dominated the Austrian operatic fashion.

For the composers of our group, however, Italy had lost most of its attraction: only Vogler, Clementi, Viotti, and Cherubini had studied there — and the last two only because they were native Italians. There are only two opera composers worth consideration in our group: Cherubini and Méhul — this is at a time when success in opera was the yardstick of a composer's stature! During the three or four decades under discussion, Italian opera celebrated some of its greatest triumphs in London and Paris; but not one of our men profited by it, not even Cherubini. Obviously there is a discrepancy here. How is it to be explained that of our musicians only two amounted to anything in opera? The true reason for this situation, aside from the matter of operatic fashion, introduces one of the most consequential aspects of nineteenth-century music: namely, specialization. Most of our composers were pianists: that is, pianoforte virtuosos. I emphasize the term pianoforte here, because they wrote no longer for the clavier, the keyboard instrument in general, but specialized on the modern pianoforte. Only the oldest member of our company, Abbé Vogler, and its last and most gifted adherent, young Mendelssohn, mastered all keyboard instruments, piano, harpsichord, and organ — because both of them were fervent champions of old music. This romantic overspecialization led to the extreme case of Chopin, who in his creative output practically limited himself to one medium, the pianoforte.

Our friends do not go that far; but they also cultivate chiefly the pianoforte, and this preference determines their stylistic traits. Registering them as contemporaries by mere chronology will not lead us anywhere — we must search for common elements. And here we should take cognizance of their common dilemma: should they write music which would be played and sold, or strive for the Parnassus of high art, refusing all compromise? This was a burning problem not only for composers, but also for poets. It was again Schiller who, with unerring judgment, pointed out the sore spot. He wrote to Goethe:

Popularity, far from alleviating the artist's labors, or from covering mediocrities, constitutes an additional difficulty. The achievement of popularity is in truth so difficult a task, that its successful accomplishment may be called the highest triumph of genius. What an undertaking, to satisfy the refined taste of the connoisseur, without becoming tasteless to the mob — to accommodate oneself to the artistic sense of the people without compromising in the least the dignity of art!

About twenty years before this was written Mozart had to cope with the same problem, and, having solved it, wrote his father on December 28, 1782: "My concertos hold the middle between the extremes of too learned and too light; they are very brilliant, agreeable to listen to; this, of course, without becoming inane. Occasionally connoisseurs alone will get full satisfaction — yet in a way that the layman [*Nichtkenner*] will be pretty much content, without knowing why."

Let us take now a second look at our composers. Among them there were only two or three who did not court popularity: Cherubini, Dussek, and Louis Berger. In this respect the unyielding rock was Cherubini — and he was the only one who survived. Is that just an accident? Young Mendelssohn, on the other hand, approached the ideal of classic popularity in his "Songs without Words," and succeeded, perhaps beyond his own intentions. All the other composers of our company, however acclaimed in their day, failed to reach more than an ephemeral fame. Schiller was right; it takes genius to attain classic popularity. As a footnote we may remember that Mozart had succeeded in attaining popularity, also Beethoven in some of his works, even more so Schubert, not to speak of Haydn and Weber, the classic idols of the German *bourgeoisie.* To consider the question of what constitutes the popularity of the classics would be tantamount to a study on sets of value in music, a task which by far exceeds the scope of this paper. Yet there is little doubt that during the classic period polyphony was considered "learned" music and therefore less popular than the simple homophonic idiom of opera or the gallant style.

Indeed, the historical battleground of musical styles has usually been the issue for and against polyphony. Since the *ars nova* the question of polyphony has stood at the center of stylistic changes. The time of which we speak is no exception to the rule. The musical gazettes of the period are full of remarks about learned, original, natural, effective, etc., music. Once more the old conflict between the *stile osservato* and the *stile sueto* or *galante* was revived, and it is interesting to note that a composer, once he had declared his allegiance to one or the other of the styles, rarely left his chosen path. The only true exception to this rule is again young Mendelssohn, who mastered all these styles; but here we must bear in mind that he did not come from either the pure classic or the romantic group; his teacher Friedrich Zelter was an artist of rare independence, and, what counts more in our discussion, was not an instrumental composer at all, but a fervent vocalist.

As for the battle pro and contra polyphony, we may say that only the older members of our group mastered and used polyphonic technique. Vogler, Cherubini, Clementi, Berger, perhaps Hummel, in their solid works used contrapuntal devices regularly and with good effect. The others, if they ever tried to do it, usually failed. We encounter a number of ludicrous attempts by an otherwise fine composer such as Dussek and the less said about the contrapuntal extravaganzas of a Moscheles or Cramer, the better.

In fact, during our period the conflict was not so much between polyphony and homophony, but between brilliant music, suitable for the salon, and solid music for the music-lover — yet the *summum bonum* seemed at least to the romanticists to be "originality." How strongly this sentiment was felt by the younger generation is evident from young Wagner's fresh attack against the "learned" *Euryanthe* of poor Weber. Schlegel's word "Man's virtue consists in his originality" was a tenet for the romanticists, but not for our group. Even Mendelssohn looked upon this truly romantic ideal with a jaundiced eye — and wrote: "Das Streben nach 'neuen Bahnen' ist ein vertrackter Dämon für jeden Künstler."

Although we can find here a certain difference between the older and the younger generation, they are all good conformists when it comes to the use of established forms. Without exception they write sonata forms for larger works, monothematic or so-called characteristic pieces of smaller size, and, whenever they let themselves go for really saleable stuff, they invariably preferred the "air varié," usually on allegedly "national" melodies. This was a trend introduced by Haydn, and it had found general acclaim. The notorious Henri Herz is said to have composed more than 150 of such sets of variations. We may ridicule both the salon-variations and the national element in them, but we cannot deny that just out of this lowland of mediocrity there arose the music of Chopin. It was he who elevated the brilliance of the salon-piece to a new piano style, and also became one of the pioneers of national music.

The nonromantics, such as Cherubini the old, and Mendelssohn the young, reacted sharply against the abuse of both the variation form and the folkloristic idea. In fact, Mendelssohn wrote his "Variations sérieuses," as the title indicates, as a demonstration against the fashionable drawing-room stuff. In an unpublished letter, he says: "Ich will den Herren doch einmal zeigen was eine Harke ist" (somewhat like "I'll show them what's the real McCoy!").

Interesting in our group is the inclination to, and the playing with, cyclical ideas and concepts. Entirely unlike the programmatically intended cyclical attempts in Beethoven's great works, such as we find in his fifth and ninth symphonies, and also different in intent from the incipient leitmotif techniques of opera since Mozart's *Magic Flute* or Weber's *Freischütz*, these cyclical experiments seem to originate in the almost instinctive desire to counterbalance the dualistic elements of the sonata form by an integrating force. As far as I have been able to establish, this type of cyclical structure *without* extra-musical associations is first evident in Schubert's second symphony. There we en-

counter a clear attempt to link the trio of the Scherzo with the theme
of the second movement (Example 7).

Example 7.

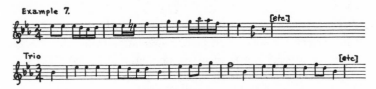

Of our group, four composers experimented frequently with cyclical
ideas: L. Berger, Dussek, Moscheles, and, of course, young Mendelssohn.
I emphasize here the "young"; for the older Felix, tamed by his wife,
became more conservative and academic every day, until the very last
year of his life, when he began to emancipate himself from his wife's
influence — and then it was too late. But in his youth, he experimented
a good deal with cyclical structures, as you may see in his A minor
and E-flat major quartets, in his octet, in his juvenile fantasy-sonata in
B-flat, and in some unpublished works.

Dussek toyed with such conceptions in his fine and undeservedly
forgotten G minor piano concerto, and in some of his sonatas. Moscheles implemented the idea firmly and clearly in his *Concerto patetico*.

The most radical step in the direction of cyclical form was taken by
Louis Berger, Mendelssohn's piano teacher. This shy introvert hit upon
the idea of constructing an entire sonata upon one motif — and he carried out his idea in his Sonata in C Minor (op. 18) on the motif shown
in Example 8.

Example 8.

A serious contemporary critic, Ludwig Rellstab, had this to say about
the revolutionary work, which appeared in 1834 or 1835, but was already
conceived in its first form in 1816:

This is a masterpiece of contrapuntal technique, in the manifold use of
the motif, which appears in augmented, diminished, inverted shape and
is constantly varied rhythmically — in addition it is full of phantastic imag-

ination. Altogether it represents a cordial accord of industry and imagination.

Berger was a disciple of Muzio Clementi and had absorbed his teacher's new ideas of pianistic style. Harmonically, however, Berger and his generation were much more conservative than either the late Clementi or Mozart, not to mention the mature Schubert. The ideal tone quality (*Das Klangideal*) which our group tried to achieve, or to emulate, was that of Mozart, not that of Beethoven; needless to add that even Hummel, Mozart's personal disciple, never did fully attain it. The romanticists strove toward a mixed orchestra, extremely flexible in its nuances, less standardized but "original" and "individualistic," and did not hesitate, occasionally, to break the balance of the traditional, homogeneous orchestra. In this respect, and mainly there, Mendelssohn reacted as a romanticist.

Mustering the members of our group individually, we shall have to admit that we find among them only three composers of truly high standard, and all three of them must be associated with the classic school rather than the romantic. They are Cherubini, Clementi, and young Mendelssohn — all three artists, not artisans, all three also reflecting inventors, not at all naïve. None the less, a combination of naïve genius with true art was still possible during the nineteenth century, as is proved by the case of Anton Bruckner.

It is regrettable that for reasons of time limit I can no more than mention the remarkable figure of Anton Reicha, one of the most original theorists and writers of the nineteenth century. He championed some bold concepts of harmony and toyed even with abandoning strict tonality, foreseeing quarter-tone music. Perhaps nowhere can we better behold that Janus-faced era than by juxtaposing with Reicha's revolutionary theories, which lead to the frontiers of tonality, a statement about the composer Viotti, written by his biographer Eymar in 1826:

Il est profonde dans la science de l'harmonie, versé, non seulement dans l'enchainment des accords, des phrases musicales, et *partout dans la succession naturelle* des accens passionés. . . .[2]

[2] J. Eymar, *Anecdotes sur Viotti* (Paris, 1826).

The writer was a fervent admirer of J. J. Rousseau's ideas.

If we now summarize our findings, we arrive at the following main results:

1. The rise of the *grande* and *petite bourgeoisie* determined not only the social status of the composer, but also the shift from classical-minded Vienna to the Berlin-Paris-London axis.

2. The cleavage between artist and artisan widens deeply during our period and becomes generally understood.

3. Most composers of our group may properly be termed mannerists in the broadest sense of this term. They are compromisers between the classic and the romantic schools, and also between the ideals of high art and easy popularity. Only those who renounced the ephemeral fashion survived.

4. This small elite became aware of the increasing dilemma of how to satisfy both the mutually exclusive postulates of personal originality and a homogeneous style. In this sense they functioned as the bridge between classicism and romanticism, but they never had insight or homogeneity enough to form a tradition of their own.

After the disappearance of our group, the universalism of the classic school was rejected *en bloc*, and yet it was classicism which, almost unintentionally, had created the most powerful and characteristically national works of art. In its place the national ego was celebrated, which has to distinguish itself from all other nations and aspires to outclass them. The old unity of European art disintegrated; our group, however ephemeral some of its members may have been, still stood for Europe as a whole.

DISCUSSION

Panelists: Nathan Broder, Donald J. Grout, Carleton Sprague Smith

Mr. Broder: I wonder if the criteria which caused you to choose this particular group of men could be extended to include two other figures: Luigi Boccherini, in the older group, and John Field among the younger men. It seems to me that both of these men have as much right in this transitional group as any that you have put there. It is true that Boccherini had nothing much to do with London or Paris, and that John Field, although he was in London for a while, spent most of his time in Russia; nevertheless, in every other respect that I can think of, they seem to belong with the men you have mentioned. They add to the interest of the group, moreover, in that Boccherini, although an Italian, had almost nothing to do with opera, and was not a pianist either. Yet, like the other older members of the group, he was capable of writing very skillful counterpoint when he chose.

Professor Werner: We can make a deal: I will accept Boccherini, but not Field. Field is a romanticist. He writes nocturnes — not *serenate notturne* — but true nocturnes; and the nocturne, for solo instrument with or without accompaniment, is a typically romantic creation. Field's *Klangideal*, moreover, approaches even more closely than that of Dussek to the mixed sound of the romantic orchestra: from Field to Chopin is only a step.

Mr. Broder: But, if you are going to draw such lines as these, I think you would have to say that Méhul, too, is too close to the romanticists to belong in your group.

Professor Werner: In his instrumental music (I refer chiefly to his two symphonies) Méhul is a strict classicist. It is true that he also plays with the idea of cyclic forms, but he does not achieve it in as radical a way as Berger,[3] Mendelssohn, or Schubert.

Mr. Broder: Still, in the opera *Joseph* of Méhul, there are two entr'actes, of which the first is a real romantic character-piece, and the second is like the finale of a Mendelssohn symphony. Material, orchestration, and pattern are typical of the early romantic period.

Professor Werner: I did not consider opera in my paper. Naturally, in opera, every entr'acte must present a new picture: that is its purpose.

Dr. Sachs: I am very much afraid that we are swimming toward a definition of classicism and romanticism. This, I think, we should avoid.

[3] In the C minor piano sonata, op. 18, referred to above, p. 63.

Professor Grout: I am sorry to hear you say so, as I had been about to ask on what criteria a composer would be judged a romantic.

Professor Werner: I would not know. I could not give you a definition of either "classic" or "romantic"; and the mere idea that such a definition is possible comes from that curious ontological belief that everything which exists is capable of definition, and that, conversely, everything which is incapable of definition does not, *ipso facto*, exist. This latter, of course, is patent nonsense, for "law," "justice," "truth" — all these philosophical ideas which are not capable of definition — would not exist according to such a theorem. I can use terms like "classic" and "romantic" only as dialectical conveniences.

Professor Grout: I ask for this reason: as the field of musicology is currently laid out, with clearly defined boundary lines, we must classify as transitional any composer or group of composers who comes after one "important" movement and before another "important" movement. Now these composers we have been discussing are, in that sense, transitional; between classicism and romanticism. But how can we say they are transitional between two things when we can define neither of them?

Professor Werner: It is to evade this difficulty that I propose the terms: "Vienna school," and "Paris-Leipzig-Berlin axis."

Professor Grout: But are we not then constituting the group on solely geographical grounds?

Professor Werner: On "geo-musical" grounds.

Professor Grout: Then what I am interested in is the musical character of that axis.

Professor Werner: I seriously doubt, speaking from my studies of these men, that we can set down strict common denominators, without using Procrustean methods.

Professor Grout: Are not all methods Procrustean? We cannot speak of history as a mere undifferentiated stream of events: we must have some sort of methods — Procrustean if you wish — to make sense of it.

Professor Werner: This, in the Hegelian sense, would be philosophy of history. But that is a philosophical problem. . . .

Dr. Landon: I should like to observe that the lines between classicism and romanticism are much more vague than people generally realize. It is perfectly obvious, at the end of Haydn's and Mozart's careers, where they were leading: toward the romanticism which their successors carried on. One of the manifestations of the vagueness of the line is the treatment of cyclical forms which Dr. Werner mentioned. I think that there is very strong evidence of cyclical tendencies in, for instance, the Mozart "Jupiter" Symphony, in some of the Haydn Masses, and, particularly, in a Clementi symphony which he wrote in London in 1794. Of this, the *London Morning Chronicle* says, with some astonishment, that the third movement has the same *cantus firmus* as the second, except that it is twice as fast. Naturally, cyclical forms did not suddenly spring forth full grown, but appeared very gradually on the scene. There are traces of them in Handel, and Bach, and the great symphonic works of Haydn or Mozart are cyclical insofar as one cannot take the last movement of one symphony and simply transpose it to make a suitable finale for another. I do not believe, as some do, that these works are based on a single thematic element, but I am sure that they have an essential thematic unity.

Dr. Smith: It seems to me that one must go to individual works, and not generalize too much about a composer's entire output. Often it is easy enough to make out a case for classicism or romanticism on the basis of a single work, but impossible to support the same opinion about the rest of a composer's music. Thus Hummel was doubtless dominated by the piano, but one certainly does not feel this in his string quartets. Or, again, take the string quartets of Viotti, which are quite contrapuntal; or the C minor sonata of Berger which you mentioned, which may well not be typical of Berger's usual music. If Dr. Sachs would like a summing-up, I should say that we are in much the same position as we are in regard to the contemporaries of Haydn: we simply do not know enough yet about the individuals.

Dr. Sachs: We have heard warnings — against specialization and individualization on the one hand (from Professor Grout) and against sweeping generalizations on the other (from Dr. Werner and Mr. Smith). I think there is not a single part of our science, or of any other science, where one does not have to steer between the same Scylla and Charybdis. If we lose ourselves in too exact individualizations, we make history stop. Nor can we consider man without his environment, without his heritage, nor without his legacy. As long as possible, we should avoid all "isms," whether on one side or the other.

It seems to me that Dr. Werner did not intend to make an antithesis between classicism and romanticism; and I think — in view of the fact that the last book on romanticism that I know of registers more than two hundred definitions of the term — we should not try to make definitions. We should merely recognize the fact that there were groups of composers whose work showed opposing elements — and whether these were elements of classicism or romanticism matters less. What does matter is that we should study these secondary figures (I am not going to call them transitional), and not harp always on the same few great names.

PROBLEMS OF INTONATION
IN THE PERFORMANCE OF
CONTEMPORARY MUSIC

Walter Piston

It is the common everyday expressions we use in talking about music that seem to be the hardest to explain. When we hear a concert by the Pasquier Trio, to take an example that comes easily to mind, we think how superbly in tune everything is, and we feel no doubt that we can and do recognize perfection of intonation in their playing. Yet who is able to describe this "playing in tune"? Does the exactness of pitch of each tone coincide with a standard determined by the science of acoustics? Can the being in tune be tested by mechanical means? Or does the human body or spirit react to the right pitch in an unmistakable way? Replies to these and similar questions usually end, "I don't know, but I can tell by ear when it sounds in tune." It is characteristic of the art of music that so important an element as intonation can be appraised by ear and can be at the same time so elusive of definition.

We know that a musical tone made by the vibration of a string or an enclosed column of air is really a composite of tones sounding together. This is the result of the phenomenon of vibration, whereby the string or air vibrates not only in total length, but also in fractional lengths — halves, thirds, fourths, fifths, etc. Since shortening the length raises the pitch proportionately we have a chord of superposed intervals constantly diminishing in size, in the ratio of 1:2:3:4:5, etc. This is the harmonic series, sometimes fondly called the chord of nature, and it is common belief that it is from this series that the tones of our musical language were derived. One should add that the tone is identified by the lowest, and ordinarily strongest, tone of the series, called the fundamental.

It is not the purpose of this paper to attempt an exposition of acoustic theories regarding pitch, but rather to direct attention to some problems bearing on and rising from present instrumental practice. The three most important systems of standardization are familiar to music theory. The Pythagorean system, based on a pure, mathematical third harmonic (the perfect fifth), presents difficulties in tonal harmony, in that its twelfth fifth, B-sharp, is seriously out of tune with C-natural, a difference referred to as the Pythagorean comma. The system known as just intonation is based on pure fifths and thirds, but with two different major seconds, C to D, D to E. It produces fine sounds in major triads, but prohibits modulation. The third system is that of equal temperament, dividing the octave in twelve equal semitones.

When two tones are played together, they sound in tune when their harmonics agree in pitch and reinforce one another. This state of affairs is of comparatively rare occurrence in actual ensemble music, and it represents but one kind of being in tune. More often the harmonics, or overtones, from lower notes are dissonant with the sounds of upper voices. Another sometimes audible result of playing two tones together is the difference tone, sounding at a pitch represented by the mathematical difference between the frequencies of the two. Violinists sometimes listen for difference tones as a test of the purity of double-stops.

Now it is safe to say that performing musicians have, with exceedingly few exceptions, little or no knowledge of these physical matters of pitch. Who has heard of a violin teacher exercising his pupil in Pythagorean intonation as contrasted with just intonation, or in the problems of equal-temperament tuning? In justice to them it may be pointed out that, while it is probably true that our musical tones are derived from harmonics of a fundamental tone, it is also true that the chord of nature finds a qualified acceptance in practice. The seventh harmonic is summarily rejected as being too flat to use. The four successive major seconds — seventh to eighth, eighth to ninth, ninth to tenth, and tenth to eleventh harmonics — are obviously each smaller than the one preceding, yet everyone thinks of the major second as having a standard size. And there is more trouble higher up.

Under these conditions one wonders how string and wind players ever learn to play in tune. The process is evidently one of imitating one's teacher and other good players, reliance being placed on that same mysterious faculty by which listeners detect flaws in intonation. In some instruction a few principles may be advanced. Classes in solfeggio may be introduced to the comma of Pythagoras in differentiating between G-sharp and A-flat. Teachers of stringed instruments may explain that major thirds and leading tones are to be played high, and that tendency tones should be flattened or sharpened in the direction of their destinations.

The performer more or less gradually acquires a sense of intonation, of hearing whether or not his tones are in tune with one another, and in tune with tones played by other performers. Individuals vary in the capacity to play in tune and we say that one has better intonation than another, thus suggesting that being in tune may be a variable quality. Some acquire or may be gifted with what we call absolute pitch, an infallible memory for sounds represented by written notes, often a not unmixed blessing where flexibility is concerned. In any event, it cannot be said that the principles learned are based on any scientific method of pitch measurement, but rather they are handed on by means of imitation and criticism.

In ensemble performance the adjustment of one's own pitch is instinctive, automatic, and usually unconscious. It is also continuous, and the result is a perpetual, though sometimes minute, fluctuation in the over-all pitch of a group of instruments. A player reacts to the sounds of others and adjusts to them even when he feels he is right.

The layman does not realize that performers on wood-wind and brass instruments are fully as preoccupied with playing in tune as are string players. It is not enough that the proper combination of open and closed tone-holes is taken, or the right valve depressed. Almost every harmonic in the overtone series has to be approached with suspicion and carefully managed by the lips to sound in tune.

It is said that a string quartet sounds in tune because it plays "in the pure scale." Whatever is meant by the pure scale, the fact is that an organized string quartet achieves a superior perfection of intonation only through years of constant rehearsing and playing together.

Dr. Charles Shackford, in his dissertation entitled "Intonation in Ensemble String Performance," [1] brought out, by the analysis of sound waves, photographically recorded on microfilm during the performance of specially prepared musical phrases, that players made considerable revision of intonation between the first sight-reading of a passage and the second or third reading, when they got to appreciate the melodic and harmonic significance of all the notes. This, together with our foregoing observations, would seem to support the notion of a musical meaning, a strictly musical meaning existing only in musical terms and essential to the communicative power of music.

Let us for a moment imagine we are at the opera, a performance of *Tristan*, and that during the first entr'acte we are interviewing people in the foyer, asking the question, "What does the first chord in the prelude mean to you?"

First we meet a jeweled and haughty dowager who answers, "Young man, how dare you!"

Then a charming young lady who murmurs, "I was in a boat — a dream boat!"

And then, of course, there's the Harvard undergraduate: "Ah yes! Very interesting. That second bassoon. He was nearly a comma sharp, threatening for an instant the key of G-flat major."

A Radcliffe junior interrupts: "That would only be five of two, enharmonically."

"Not a chance," says the Harvard man. "The extra high G-sharp appoggiatura of the oboe made it quite unnecessary to await the resolution of A to understand that we were in a supertonic augmented six-four-three."

Evidently the first two interviewed were thinking of other than strictly musical meanings. Of course meaning, in purely musical terms, goes deeper than dry technical description of melodic and harmonic

[1] Harvard, 1954.

processes. Moreover, the listener need not be able to explain the musical meaning he perceives, especially if he is not a musician.

At the present time, musical meaning is by common usage pretty thoroughly grounded in major-minor tonal feeling, for both performers and listeners, so that patterns are seen, played, and heard in relation to a tonality, either the right one or a hypothetical one. The tonal feeling is made stronger in performance by nuances of intonation. The effect is a clearer communication of the music's message, except when that message is not concerned with major-minor tonality, in which case there is bound to be a distortion of the composer's meaning.

It is plain that perception of musical meaning on the part of the performer is a prerequisite for playing in tune. But one may ask if this musical meaning can exist apart from conventional tonal feeling. And does it so exist in the practice of performers when playing nontonal music?

The education of an instrumentalist normally consists of the practicing of studies and pieces whose musical meaning lies solidly within a well-established common language. While this language contains plenty of intonational problems, even some insoluble ones, he manages to learn by listening to others to play acceptably in tune, given the advantage of a generous pitch tolerance possessed by the listener. In a contemporary idiom, such as twelve-tone music, for example, his judgment of intonation being based on tonal feeling, the average string or wind player will either be quite lost, or he will unwittingly contribute a sense of major-minor tonality foreign to the intent of the music. Even in music less contemporary in language, if tonal aspects are not readily discernible, extra rehearsing and study become necessary, and complaints are voiced that the music is written in a needlessly complex way. "Why write F-flat? That's E." And double sharps are often changed to their enharmonic equivalents, by editors as well as performers.

One need not go outside the common harmonic practice of the nineteenth century to encounter problems that have no satisfactory solution. Numerous chords, like the diminished seventh, cannot be tonally oriented until the next chord is heard, and perhaps not then; and in an enharmonic modulation it is obviously impossible for all the tones to be in tune both going and coming.

Instinctive reaction by the performer to the tonal meaning of harmony was demonstrated in an experiment by the writer, in which a double-bass player was asked to hold an A-flat while the remaining notes of the dominant seventh of the key of E-flat major were played above on the piano. Then, while he held the tone, the notes E-natural, B-natural, and D were substituted above, showing his note to be now G-sharp, leading tone of A major. He was clearly seen, as well as heard, to move to an appreciably higher pitch, but he emphatically denied that it was anything more than a correction of the A-flat, which he felt was out of tune. This experiment was the more remarkable in that the piano itself was not well tuned.

Musical meaning also gives rise to what may be called subjective aspects of intonation. A diminished fifth is played on the piano, the lower tone being recognized as a leading tone. With a little concentration the interval may be changed mentally to an augmented fourth, whereupon the upper tone seems to have risen in pitch. Of course, the pitch has not changed physically but the meaning of the interval has changed, and that change has been perceived, probably in terms of tonal implication.

Everyone does not own up to this kind of sensitivity, and some may be satisfied to call it merely recognition of musical meaning. It is induced by intelligent and musical piano playing, when all the notes seem to be presented in their true values and relationships, and it provides a basis in reason for the remark about a certain pianist — "He plays the piano in tune."

The phenomenon of subjective pitch change is rather closely related to the important phenomenon of pitch tolerance. This tolerance comes into play when musical meaning is communicated. For example, a dominant seventh chord with its resolution to its tonic may be played on the most frightfully out-of-tune piano and everyone will understand this most familiar of musical words. Some would doubtless be able to write the notes heard — or we might say assumed to have been heard.

Our pitch tolerance is now such that not only do we perceive musical meaning when music is quite badly out of tune, but also we do not seem to be aesthetically disturbed by bad intonation as long as we detect musical meaning. Since most music we hear is more or less out of tune this might seem to be a good thing. It is undeniably a good thing, even indispensable, when we listen to piano music. But in other music pitch tolerance, with its accompanying tendency to find patterns of meaning of a well-established and familiar nature, may prove to be a factor in the loss of higher aesthetic values, and the reduced ability to perceive finer nuances of musical meaning. Furthermore, it appears as a force operating against the reception of new developments. It is ironical that this wide tolerance of pitch, which enables us to endure without too much discomfort a concert by an amateur chorus or instrumental group, should at the same time act as an obstacle to the understanding of music that does not follow well-known patterns, and should be actually a hindrance to the evolution of musical language.

What of equal temperament in all this? The pianoforte is assumed to be tuned in equal temperament. But it is tuned by a human being, the piano tuner. He uses no scientific apparatus to make certain of the equality of the twelve semitones. On the contrary, he uses shaded Pythagorean fifths and fourths, and his major thirds may answer only to his own taste. And anyway, the piano does not stay in tune for long.

When other instruments play with the piano they adjust to it when necessary, in the same way they adjust to any instrument, but they follow their tonal instincts at those moments when they are not hampered by the piano part. The listener exercises pitch tolerance here, and also subjective interpretation of pitch. No doubt it would be possible to achieve equal temperament by electronic means, but in current instrumental practice it may be said to exist in theory only.

New problems face the performer of twentieth-century music, that is, unless it be music by composers who by unawareness or inclination have remained outside the evolutionary currents of our musical language. Most of the problems have to do with tonality. Some music is clearly tonal. Some is vaguely or fleetingly tonal. Some is tonal despite the composer's wish to write in an atonal idiom. Some verges on atonality despite the composer's constant thought of a tonal center.

And some reaches an advanced level of atonality. By and large, the performers are not prepared to follow these developments, especially since the melodic and harmonic material of the new music, even that which is clearly tonal, may be unfamiliar, and may at first appear to be without musical meaning.

It is perhaps not so much that the problems are new, but that the approach to them is hampered by established and instinctive playing habits. The question of what to do in an enharmonic change is only a little more complex than in the playing of a whole-tone scale. A chord of superposed fourths presents several possibilities of tonal meaning, but perhaps not more than a simple triad out of context. An unresolved appoggiatura needs the same melodic inflections and rhythmic leaning that it would have if resolved. Modes and scales other than major and minor have been used by composers all along, but in the twentieth century there has been an enormous expansion of these resources, and it goes without saying that the intonational problems are many and varied, and are in need of study and clarification.

The second quarter of the twentieth century has seen the spread of the philosophy and principles of twelve-tone technique to the extent that very few composers of our day have escaped the influence of this movement. Their reaction to its influence varies from positive acceptance to negative rejection. It is just this variation that poses the most difficult question for the performer. A new element is slowly but surely becoming by increasing usage a part of our musical language, calling for perception of a musical meaning much wider in scope than that recognized by most players.

The principles, or rules, of twelve-tone composition are, like any other principles of the art of music, still in the making, and any declared set of rules seems destined for modification or even destruction by the subsequent practice of composers. Two of these principles are of very serious concern to performers seeking to play in tune. The first is the generally accepted idea that the twelve tones are of equal importance and that no one tone is to be allowed to assume the role of tonic or dominant. Experience and a little perspective have shown that tonal feeling is present in much music of even the most prominent exponents or adherents of the twelve-tone system. Again it must be emphasized that tonal feeling may exist in degrees varying from little or none to unquestionably absolute. The line between tonality and atonality in actual music is far from sharp.

The other principle is that twelve-tone music is to be written in equal temperament. When this procedure has been observed, the performer is called upon to be able to recognize the fact, and then to play his notes according to equal temperament tuning. This requires vastly more knowledge on his part, and also the ability to achieve complete freedom from long-standing habits.

The problem for the player is reflected in the practice of composers in respect to the notation of twelve-tone music. Most composers try to give melodic outlines a look of naturalness and readability, and this again takes on a look of tonal meaning. Attempts to avoid this tonal appearance produce combinations of intervals bewildering to the player, and when he has worked out a method of performing the passage he will have interpreted some notes enharmonically, and he will in effect have rewritten the music more or less tonally.

Inquiries among musicians who have given notable performances of twelve-tone music and of other modern music requiring a negation of conventional tonal meaning have turned up no information pointing to a methodical approach to playing this music in tune, other than, "We practice it until we know it together, and until it sounds to us in tune." This brings us right back to our opening paradox. We know when music is in tune but we do not know what this is that we know.

This brief survey cannot but end with a recapitulation of suggested and unanswered queries.

Why do we not accept pitches given by nature? And why do we pretend we do?

Is nicety of pitch essential to our understanding and enjoyment of music?

Will we ever be able to narrow pitch tolerance to the point where we can perceive and understand music using intervals smaller than the minor second?

Is it possible or desirable to learn to play in equal temperament?

Can the notation of music be improved to the extent of being able to indicate equal-temperament tuning?

Does the dilemma created by those two unscientific and very important phenomena, pitch tolerance and musical meaning, imply that the art of music has reached an impasse and that no further developments in language are possible?

Would performance by electronic instruments of perfect pitch prove satisfying, considering the value of pitch inflection in intensifying musical meaning?

Is it true that pitch tolerance may be increasing in breadth as a result of indiscriminate use of phonograph records?

How can the teaching of instrument playing include these various aspects of intonation?

Or, as final thought, shall we not, as musicians, take satisfaction in contemplating one more demonstration of the versatility, the flexibility, the richness, the indescribable mystery, and the inescapable communicative power of all combinations of musical sounds?

DISCUSSION

Panelists: Egon Kenton, Otto Luening, Arthur Mendel

Professor Kenton: My first point concerns the allegation that "nature" has given us pitches:[2] here I differ from the speaker. It seems to me that nature has never given us any pitches at all, but rather an infinite glissando of tones, exactly like a spectrum. From this glissando we have picked out certain nuances of color — nuances of pitch — and, in different periods, created various tonal systems, whether modal, pentatonic, heptatonic, twelve-tone, or whatever. Naturally we cannot exactly adjust a complex of different tones to each other, because they are arbitrarily chosen from an infinite series.

Furthermore, in music such as that of Debussy and Ravel, we encounter varying applications of different tonal systems in the same piece: modal, pentatonic, and heptatonic. Yet we perform these pieces on instruments which are adapted to only one of these systems.

[2] See above, p. 70 and below, p. 80.

Performers are, as Professor Piston pointed out, generally unaware that such problems exist: they merely try to make the music sound as much in tune as their best knowledge permits. But their best knowledge is tainted by their musical education, which, even today, at the mid-point of the twentieth century, is largely devoted to tonal music. Still, I know from my own experience that performers do spend a very large part of their rehearsal time on intonation, and that they are not satisfied until they come up with something which they believe is good. This is perhaps the main thing.

Even tonal music presents difficulties. At first one might think that musicians of the early seventeenth century might have been the least troubled, since their harmonies consisted mainly of the same few chords; but even they had to use the supertonic and the third degree, so that their position was hardly better. My remarks, therefore, are anarchistic: Nature gives us an unending series of pitches, and we pick from among them an arbitrary series, which we then find we cannot really use.

Aside from this, I will make only one remark: when a musician says, "Why write F-flat when you mean E?" this is not because of his tonal hearing, but because it is easier to finger as E.

Professor Piston: A member of the Boston Symphony Orchestra told me that there was no fingering for F-flat on a violin. There seems to be a campaign against using something so difficult to read as F-flat.

Incidentally, I did not say that we got our tone series from nature, but that it was commonly believed that we got them from nature.

Professor Luening: I should like to add a few things in the nature of footnotes to Professor Piston's paper. In the first place, one may include in the list of elements that affect intonation the whole matter of present-day concert practice: the kind of halls used, the temperature of the halls, and the seating arrangement of the musicians. You can have a very precise intonation worked out in rehearsal, and, if in performance the hall temperature is only a few degrees warmer, the strings will be down and the winds up. The best-planned intonation is then ruined . . . by the janitor. Still, even under these conditions, music survives.

It is only when a combination of these factors seriously affects the pitch approximation that the performance and consequently the effect of the music suffer.

Seating arrangement is important. It seems to me that a standard seating arrangement, that would suit all contemporary music, is probably impossible. In certain large areas of music, in which the strings are the carriers of the main musical ideas, the orchestra must be arranged so that the string sections are in close communication. In much contemporary music, however, the play back and forth among the winds is extremely important, and in such cases, the seating arrangement cannot simply be left to some standard practice.

One other thing that affects intonation in contemporary music is the mania for raising the pitch of the A. By raising it from 436 as far as 444, the winds, especially, get into a range where it is impossible to have any control over the pitch of the higher notes: the lip simply cannot do it, even though the ear demands it.

Musical meaning, moreover, insofar as this gives clues to playing in tune, is not merely a question of external things — of the hope and intention of playing in tune — but of internal things as well. This idea of meaning in contemporary music needs to be brought up for accurate study in our educational institutions. I am inclined to think that such a course would simplify the problems in classical and romantic music as well.

It has already been pointed out that one of the problems in contemporary music is that various wind instruments are built in different keys — horns in F, clarinets in B-flat, and so on — and are thus inherently unsuitable for twelve-tone music. This presents a real problem for the performers, and one which they do not understand, since they have no idea what is the matter. They wonder why, in a twelve-tone piece for B-flat clarinet, D-flat piccolo, and a stringed instrument, they cannot "lean" the tone over enough to get in tune; and they do not realize that their instrument simply cannot do it in this sort of music.

There are, as Mr. Piston pointed out, some scientific ways of helping to achieve scientific precision. With an audio-oscillator one can now reconstruct any modes, any scales, any micro-scales, or any combinations desired. These reconstructions may be used as exact measuring sticks, either for educational or for aesthetic purposes. Certainly, in micro-tonal and twelve-tone music, it is possible, with the aid of electronic instruments, to do what Stockhausen, Boulez, and others have done: write music which is extremely precise and in tune, and yet goes through a very great aural range. The question then arises: how much of this can the ear absorb? Is there not a limit to the possible complexity, both harmonically and melodically?

Professor Mendel: Several of us seem to have been caught by the fact that we once took a more active interest in a subject than we do now: Dr. Hertzmann in the basse dance, Mr. Strunk in Haydn, and I in pitch. I might say that I retired from pitch studies about 1859, when the *diapason normal* was established. Since then there has been much less variation in the aspect of pitch — namely pitch level — which I had investigated.

Mr. Luening said something about the perpetual raising of the pitch, and, since this is one of my hobbies, I shall ride it for a moment — to point out that this is an absolute myth. Pitch has not gone steadily up, nor has it varied greatly. To go back no farther than 1857: in that year Steinway was tuning concert pianos to A equals 457. Today, with the various electronic means that are available, even including such normal ones as radio and phonograph, pitch is probably prevented from going up any appreciable amount.

Even the most supposedly scientific investigators in these matters can occasionally be extremely naïve. One of the most prominent men in the field, and certainly the most prominent historian of pitch, was Alexander John Ellis, the translator of Helmholtz. He set up, as you know, lengthy tables of pitches at different times and places,[3] worked out with considerable caution. Unfortunately he expressed his results in vibrations and decimal fractions of vibrations, giving them an appearance of accuracy and precision which was far from Ellis's mind: he had merely set down what his arithmetic gave him. When he says, for ex-

[3] Alexander John Ellis, "On the History of Musical Pitch," *Journal of the Society of Arts* (March 5, 1880), pp. 315ff.

ample, that a pitch varied between 439.3 and 440.7, obviously the .3 and .7 are wholly irrelevant: the pitch was somewhere in the neighborhood of 440, and no more can be said. Nevertheless, these figures are quoted in many places as if Ellis had established the exactness of every digit.

Ellis, nevertheless, had the notion that Mr. Piston mentioned in connection with string quartets,[4] that choruses sing in just intonation. He wished to establish the average voice ranges of singers in his day, in an attempt to prove pitch levels in other periods of history by adducing the relative constancy of the range of the human voice. (Incidentally, in a recent offprint from the *Berichte der Gesellschaft für Naturforschung*, I read of an attempt to establish the pitch in Athanasius Kircher's time by the pitch in which Kircher notated the call of the cuckoo). . . .

Professor LaRue: This ornithological approach should be discouraged. I have recently had a correspondence with an ornithologist, who tells me that the variation in pitch among various individuals of the same species is so great that the bird call cannot be relied upon as a guide for fixing pitch.

Professor Mendel: . . . Ellis's method for determining voice range (without elaborate means for pitch-determination, which were not available) was to start the chorus with a fork of known frequency, and then to have them go up by half steps until they had to stop. Each singer noted his individual stopping point, and that constituted his range.[5] Now anyone who has worked with a chorus, and imagines that the singers can go up by half steps, and, by the twelfth half step, be anywhere near an octave from the start, is absurdly naïve. Pitches that are arrived at by this means may well be out by a tone or a tone and a half.

I should like to disagree somewhat with something Mr. Luening said. Although I know that physical theory says that with rising temperature strings go down and winds go up, my experience has been that the pitch of the whole orchestra rises during the course of the evening.

[4] Above, pp. 72–73.
[5] Ellis, p. 302, where however, this method is ascribed to Alberto Randegger. Ellis describes himself as having used a diatonic scale.

Even within a given movement, where there is no opportunity for the strings to tune higher, they simply play higher. My painful experience with an electronic organ which I used for continuo purposes is a case in point: as long as I tried to tune my organ to a pitch which the oboist gave me at the beginning of the evening, there would always be a feeling of sag whenever the organ came in. As a result, I had to tune the organ higher than the oboe, because, as the evening progressed, the general pitch would rise. The instruments then had to strain a bit to get up to the higher pitch at first, but were quite comfortable with it later on.

My last question is this: what happens in pieces for string quartet (I am thinking especially of the introduction to Beethoven's opus 59, no. 3) whose whole effect depends on a series of enharmonic surprises and uncertainties? Here I should think that the effect Mr. Schackford speaks about,[6] that musicians reading a piece play it one way, and, having practiced, play it another, would work greatly to the disadvantage of the music. Once the players have realized that the diminished seventh chord F-sharp–A–C–E-flat is going to resolve (apparently) to a B-flat chord, and is thus really A–C–E-flat–G-flat, they will play the notes according to their destinations, and eventually will forget that there are any surprises at all. All but the most thoughtful will finally think that the whole introduction is perfectly straightforward, and thus the whole expressive and semantic purpose of this section will be missed.

Professor Piston: The players cannot win in any case, for if they realize where the first chord is going, the second chord will be wrong.

Professor Kenton: Similarly, in every performance and recording of the César Franck quartet, the pitch rises during the trio of the Scherzo, when the music changes from G-flat to F-sharp.

Professor Mendel: Again, this is a piece conceived for equal temperament, and the instruments simply cannot play it as written.

[6] Above, p. 73.

Professor Werner: Do you mean to imply that, as a general rule, whenever a player feels the presence of a tendency tone, he raises the pitch if it is a leading tone, and lowers it if it has a downward tendency?

Professor Mendel: This is generally true. It is what string teachers teach, and, I believe, what they play as well.

Professor Piston: Pablo Casals makes his pupils play leading tones so close to their tones of destinations that they are practically the same note. This is a supertonal interpretation.

Professor Werner: But think of Mozart's "Dissonance" Quartet (K. 465). What would happen if that were played the way you describe? I have played the viola part myself, and I did not notice anything of the sort.

Professor Mendel: The fortunate thing is that we have such pitch tolerance that anything but an absolute unison is heard as a half tone of some sort.

Professor Luening: May I mention something concerning the 440 pitch? When I spoke of the constant rise in pitch,[7] I was referring to the twentieth century. I have a flute which I bought in Munich in 1912, tuned to 435. I played that flute in orchestras abroad, and a good deal over here. If I use it now, I cannot play in the 442 pitch, because I cannot play it that high. If I try to correct this, as a good player should, I get into an impossibly awkward position. Obviously, flutes are built higher now than they were in 1912.

Dr. Kinkeldey: Professor Piston mentioned the fact that piano tuners strive toward equal temperament, and that the results are very different, depending on the individual tuner. This difficulty has been resolved. There is a firm which will provide an electronic instrument for piano tuners, by which the tuner himself is relieved of all responsibility. He merely plugs in the electrical instrument and then presses a key for, say, A. Then he plays the A of the piano, and looks at the small screen

[7] Above, p. 81.

of the instrument. If there is any difference in frequency between the two instruments, the normally stable line on the screen begins to vibrate. He then tunes the piano A until the line is still again. This is done with each semitone of the basic octave, and the other octaves are then tuned to the electronic instrument by harmonics. The tuner does not need to think, nor to hear: a deaf person could tune a piano by this means.

CODA

I think with pleasure of the many musicological congresses I attended — in London, Paris, Vienna, Basel, New York, and elsewhere. I remember the brilliant social events, the magnificent hospitality, the exquisite performances of music, the reunion with friends. What I do not recall is the scientific results. They were drowned in the attractions planned for us, torn asunder in the often unavoidable parceling of an overfed whole in separate "sections," choked in the tedium of "read" articles, "addenda," "notes," and "contributions" to God knows what insipid topic. There was no plan, no coherence, no vital principle.

This is why I will not forget the Harvard conference of May 1957. There was just one day of proceedings, one impressive library room as the arena, one monastic vesper service as an extracurricular spice, and one informal reception. The few papers were presented by hand-picked specialists within the framework of "instrumental music" and reviewed by a few equally hand-picked discussants. There was careful planning and, to a high degree, coherence and vitality.

To fully achieve the latter two qualities, we need a still greater cohesion both of speakers and of topics, shorter speeches, and a longer discussion time. In this desideratum, I am in perfect unison with the deserving, self-effacing "producers" of the symposium, A. Tillman Merritt and John M. Ward. Thus there is nothing to add than thanking these two men as well as those who assisted in their planning and kindly asking them to continue building a center for the exchange of ideas among peers, without amusing the laymen and boring the professionals.

Curt Sachs

1. AMOROSO [BALLO FRANCESE]

Giovanni Ambrosio   Paris, Ital. 476, f. 65ᵛ

89

2. ANELLO

Domenico Paris, Ital. 972, f. 16ʳ

[Saltarello in maxurà di piva]

[movimenti]

3. BELFIORE

Domenico

Paris, Ital. 972, f. 15^r

4. BELREGUARDO

Domenico	Paris, Ital. 972, f. 7ᵛ
Giovanni Ambrosio	Paris, Ital. 476, f. 63ᵛ
Cornazano	Vatican-Cappon. 203, f. 19ʳ–19ᵛ. Mazzi, p. 19
Guglielmo	Paris, Ital. 973, f. 46ᵛ

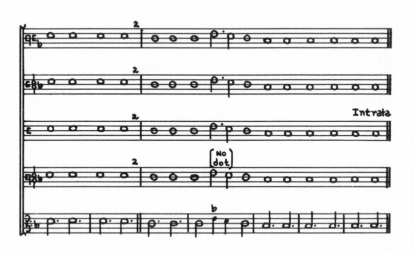

5. COLONNESE

Giovanni Ambrosio   Paris, Ital. 476, f. 64ᵛ

Guglielmo   Paris, Ital. 973, f. 50ᵛ–51ʳ

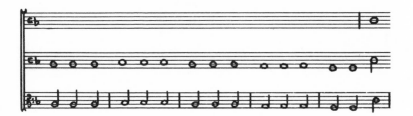

96

6. LA FIGLIA GUILIELMINO

Cornazano
Vatican-Cappon. 203, f. 23^r–
23^v. Mazzi, p. 23

Domenico
Paris, Ital. 972, f. 18^v–19^r

[Bassa danza]

[Quadernaria]

99

7. LA GELOSIA

Giovanni Ambrosio   Paris, Ital. 476, f. 63^r
Domenico   Paris, Ital. 972, f. 11^r
Guglielmo   Paris, Ital. 973, f. 47^v

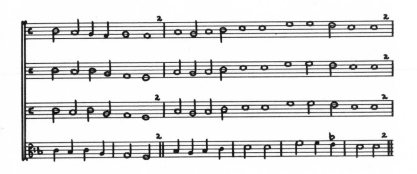

8. GIOIOSO (ROSTIBOLI GIOIOSO) in Giovanni Ambrosio
ROTI BOULLY IOYEULX in France

Brussels

Toulouze

Giovanni Ambrosio

No. 55

No. 20, f. B 1^r

Paris, Ital. 476, f. 66^r

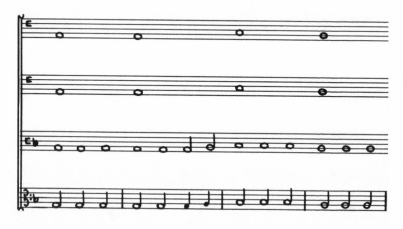

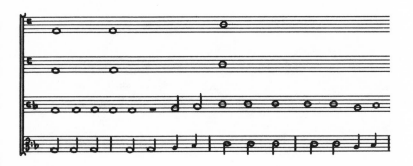

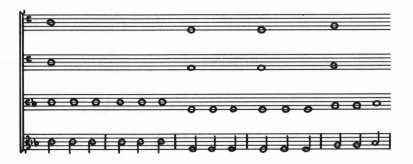

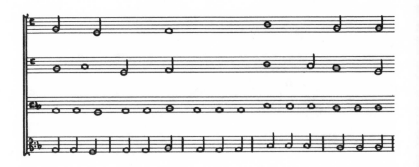

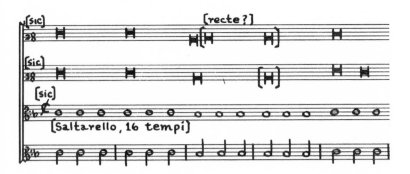

[Saltarello, 16 tempi]

105

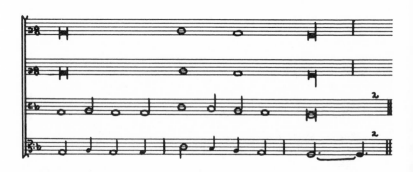

9. GIOVE (IOVE)
[= JUPITER in Domenico]

Giovanni Ambrosio	Paris, Ital. 476, f. 64ʳ
Cornazano	Vatican-Cappon. 203, f. 15ᵛ–16ʳ.
	Mazzi, p. 17.
Domenico	Paris, Ital. 972, f. 17ʳ–17ᵛ
Guglielmo	Paris, Ital. 973, f. 47ʳ–47ᵛ

10. GRATIOSO

Giovanni Ambrosio   Paris, Ital. 476, f. 62^v

Guglielmo   Paris, Ital. 973, f. 50^v

[bis dicitur]

(Piva, 3 tempi)　　　　[bis dicitur]

(Piva, 3 tempi)

(una volta)

111

11. INGRATA

Giovanni Ambrosio   Paris, Ital. 476, f. 64[r]

Domenico   Paris, Ital. 972, f. 10[r]

Guglielmo   Paris, Ital. 973, f. 48[v]–49[r]

(Saltarello)

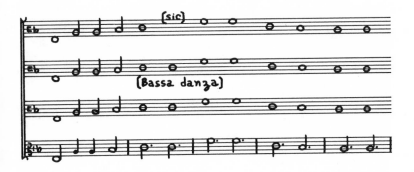

(sic)

(Bassa danza)

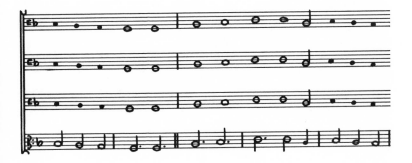

113

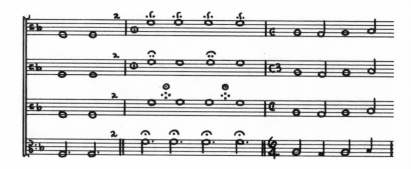

114

12. LEONCELLO

Giovanni Ambrosio   Paris, Ital. 476, f. 63^v

Cornazano   Vatican-Cappon. 203, f. 21^r,

                                Mazzi, p. 21

Domenico   Paris, Ital. 972, f. 8^v–9^r

Guglielmo   Paris, Ital. 973, f. 47^r

115

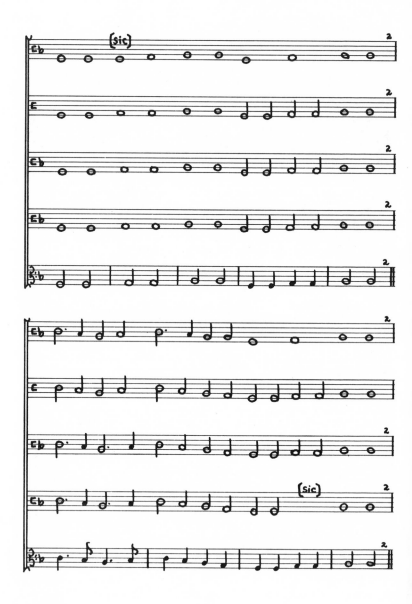

[Bassa danza]

117

13. LIGIADRA

Giovanni Ambrosio   Paris, Ital. 476, f. 65[r]

Guglielmo   Paris, Ital. 973, f. 51[r]–51[v]

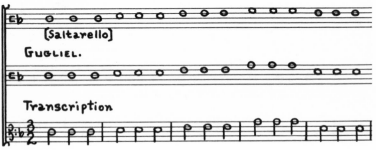

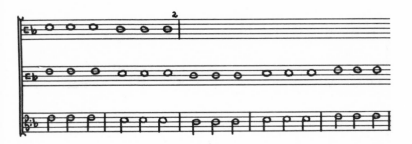

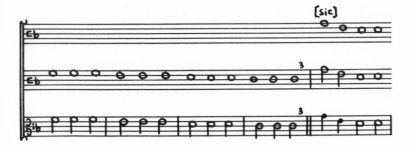

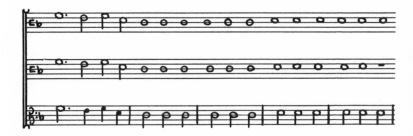

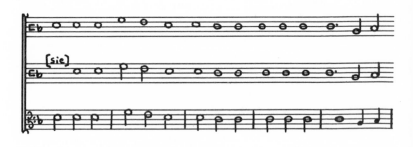

120

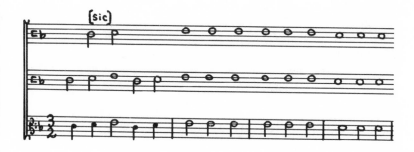

121

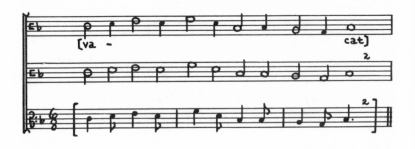

[va -   cat]

[piva]

Giovanni Ambrosio   Paris, Ital. 476, f. 62[r]

Domenico   Paris, Ital. 972, f. 16[v]

Guglielmo   Paris, Ital. 973, f. 49[v]

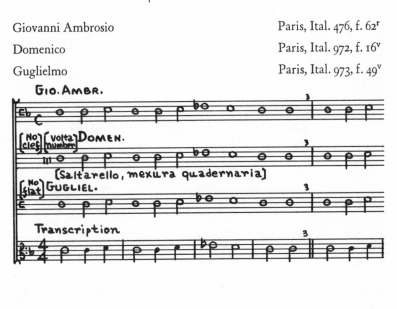

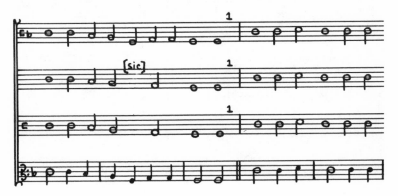

123

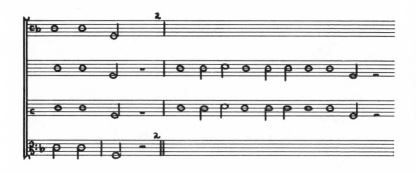

[12½ [!] tempi di bassa danza)

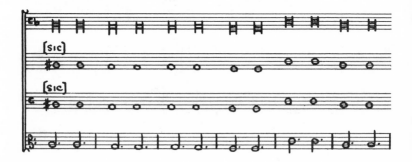

124

125

15. MERCANTIA

Giovanni Ambrosio	Paris, Ital. 476, f. 64^v
Cornazano	Vatican-Cappon. 203, f. 13^v–14^r
	Mazzi, p. 15
Domenico	Paris, Ital. 972, f. 21^r
Guglielmo	Paris, Ital. 973, f. 49^r–49^v

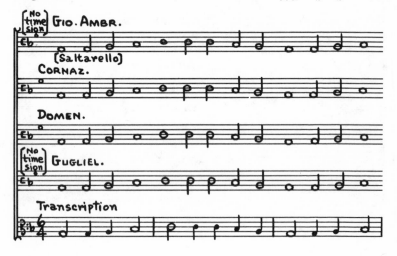

[Bassa danza]

[sic]

127

128

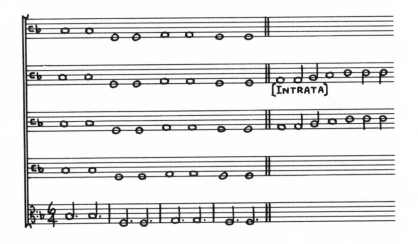

16. PETIT VRIENS
(PETIT RIENSE in tri francese)

Giovanni Ambrosio   Paris, Ital. 476, f. 65^v

129

(Piva)

130

17. LA PIZZOCARA

Giovanni Ambrosio   Paris, Ital. 476, f. 63^r

Domenico   Paris, Ital. 972, f. 12^r

Guglielmo   Paris, Ital. 973, f. 48^r–48^v

(Bassa danza)

(Saltarello)

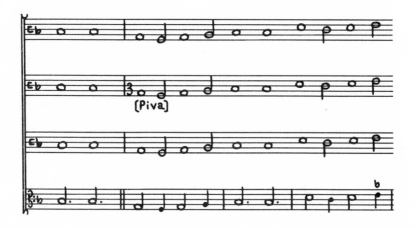

[Piva]

133

18. PRISONERA (Giovanni Ambrosio)
PREXONERA (Domenico)   PRESONIERA (Guglielmo)

Giovanni Ambrosio   Paris, Ital. 476, f. 62^v
Domenico   Paris, Ital. 972, f. 14^v
Guglielmo   Paris, Ital. 973, f. 46^r

tempi dui)

[sic]

[Saltarello todesco]

[NO sion] [Piva, tempi octo]

[Saltarello todescho, quatro tempi]

movimento movim.

[saltarello,

[saltarello)

[sic]

INTRATA

tempi quatro)

19. SOBRIA

Cornazano

Vatican-Cappon. 203, f. 26^v–27^r.
Mazzi, p. 23

Domenico

Paris, Ital. 972, f. 22^r–22^v

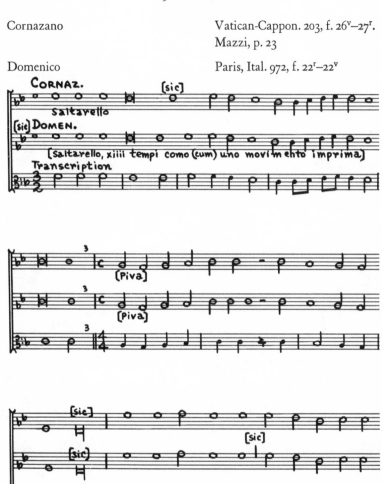

137

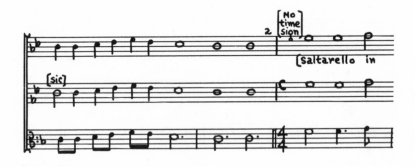

(saltarello in

quadernaria)

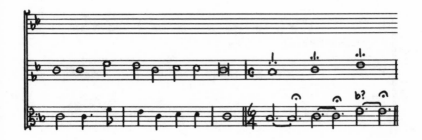

139

[Saltarello]

(Saltarello)

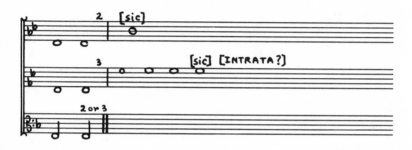

20. SPERO

Giovanni Ambrosio   Paris, Ital. 476, f. 62^r

Guglielmo   Paris, Ital. 973, f. 50^r

[Saltarello todesco]

[Saltarello todescho]

[sic]

[Saltarello]

[Saltarello]

[sic]

142

21. TESARA

Domenico Paris, Ital. 972, f. 23ᵛ–24ʳ

145

[Saltarello]

[Piva]

146

22. VERZEPPE

Cornazano

Vatican-Cappon. f. 17ᵛ–18ʳ.
Mazzi, p. 19.

Domenico

Paris, Ital. 972, f. 13ʳ

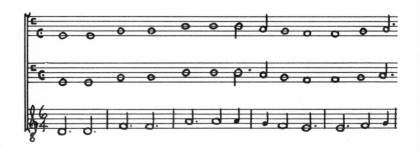

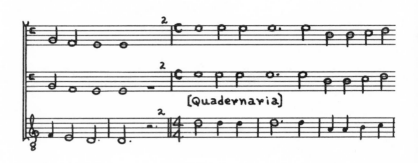

[Quadernaria]

[uno salto] [Saltarello]

148

[Bassa danza]

[saltarello] [Sic] [Bassa

danza] [Saltarello]

23. VOLTATE IN ÇA ROSINA

Giovanni Ambrosio

Paris, Ital. 476, f. 64ᵛ

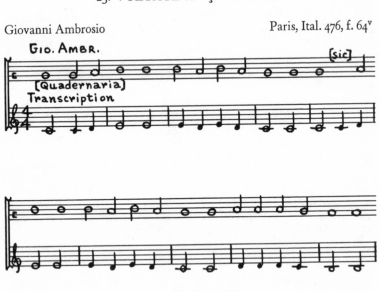

24. CORNAZANO'S BASSA DANZA AND SALTARELLO TENORS

Vatican-Cappon. 203.
Mazzi, p. 29

Tenore del Re di Spagna

= Tenor clef

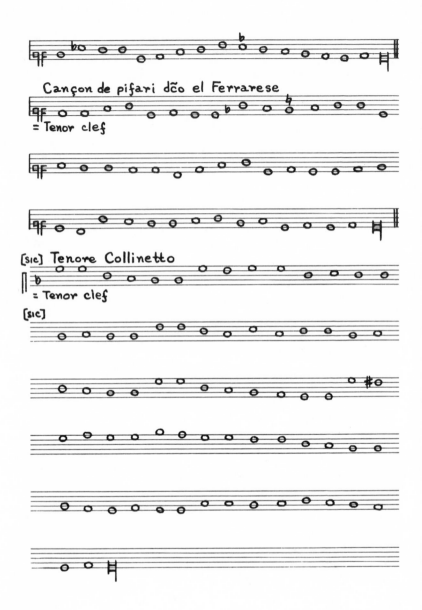

Cançon de pifari dõo el Ferrarese

= Tenor clef

[sic] Tenore Collinetto

= Tenor clef

[sic]

152